DISEASES & DISORDERS

Cancer

Elizabeth Silverthorne

LUCENT BOOKS
A part of Gale, Cengage Learning

GALE
CENGAGE Learning

Detroit • New York • San Francisco • New Haven, Conn • Waterville, Maine • London

© 2009 Gale, Cengage Learning

LIBRARY OF CONGRESS CATALOGING-IN-PUBLICATION DATA

Silverthorne, Elizabeth, 1930–
   Cancer / by Elizabeth Silverthorne.
      p. cm. — (Diseases & disorders)
   Includes bibliographical references and index.
   ISBN 978-1-4205-0113-1 (hardcover)
   1. Cancer—Juvenile literature. I. Title.
   RC264.S556 2009
   616.99'4—dc22

                                                    2008047882

Lucent Books
27500 Drake Rd.
Farmington Hills, MI 48331

ISBN-13: 978-1-4205-0113-1
ISBN-10: 1-4205-0113-5

Printed in the United States of America
2 3 4 5 6 7 13 12 11 10 09

Table of Contents

"The Most Difficult Puzzles Ever Devised"

Charles Best, one of the pioneers in the search for a cure for diabetes, once explained what it is about medical research that intrigued him so. "It's not just the gratification of knowing one is helping people," he confided, "although that probably is a more heroic and selfless motivation. Those feelings may enter in, but truly, what I find best is the feeling of going toe to toe with nature, of trying to solve the most difficult puzzles ever devised. The answers are there somewhere, those keys that will solve the puzzle and make the patient well. But how will those keys be found?"

Since the dawn of civilization, nothing has so puzzled people—and often frightened them, as well—as the onset of illness in a body or mind that had seemed healthy before. A seizure, the inability of a heart to pump, the sudden deterioration of muscle tone in a small child—being unable to reverse such conditions or even to understand why they occur was unspeakably frustrating to healers. Even before there were names for such conditions, even before they were understood at all, each was a reminder of how complex the human body was, and how vulnerable.

While our grappling with understanding diseases has been frustrating at times, it has also provided some of humankind's most heroic accomplishments. Alexander Fleming's accidental discovery in 1928 of a mold that could be turned into penicillin has resulted in the saving of untold millions of lives. The isolation of the enzyme insulin has reversed what was once a death sentence for anyone with diabetes. There have been great strides in combating conditions for which there is not yet a cure, too. Medicines can help AIDS patients live longer, diagnostic tools such as mammography and ultrasounds can help doctors find tumors while they are treatable, and laser surgery techniques have made the most intricate, minute operations routine.

This "toe-to-toe" competition with diseases and disorders is even more remarkable when seen in a historical continuum. An astonishing amount of progress has been made in a very short time. Just two hundred years ago, the existence of germs as a cause of some diseases was unknown. In fact, it was less than 150 years ago that a British surgeon named Joseph Lister had difficulty persuading his fellow doctors that washing their hands before delivering a baby might increase the chances of a healthy delivery (especially if they had just attended to a diseased patient)!

Each book in Lucent's Diseases and Disorders series explores a disease or disorder and the knowledge that has been accumulated (or discarded) by doctors through the years. Each book also examines the tools used for pinpointing a diagnosis, as well as the various means that are used to treat or cure a disease. Finally, new ideas are presented—techniques or medicines that may be on the horizon.

Frustration and disappointment are still part of medicine, for not every disease or condition can be cured or prevented. But the limitations of knowledge are being pushed outward constantly; the "most difficult puzzles ever devised" are finding challengers every day.

Cells Gone Wild

Cancer occurs when cells in the body multiply wildly and abnormally. It is a serious, frightening disease. Cancer can occur in almost any part of the human body. Most often cancers attack middle-aged and older adults, but some kinds of cancer may strike at any age.

Cancer affects people all over the world. Though not contagious, it is a common disease. More than 10 million new cases are diagnosed each year, and more than half of these victims will die from the disease. In the United States cancer is the second leading cause of death, exceeded only by heart disease. More than half a million Americans die of cancer each year. At some time in their lives, almost everyone in the country will be touched by the disease—either through their own illness or that of someone they love.

A cancer diagnosis is scary, but not nearly as scary as it was a few decades ago. In May 2008, a seventy-six-year-old man lay in a hospital bed watching his favorite baseball team, the Boston Red Sox, play the Kansas City Royals. The man was Senator Edward Kennedy, who had been admitted to the hospital for testing and would be diagnosed with brain cancer. The pitcher for the Red Sox was twenty-four-year-old Jon Lester, who had been diagnosed with non-Hodgkin's lymphoma less than two years earlier. Kennedy cheered as Lester pitched a no-hitter. In Major League Baseball history, there have been many no-hitters, but this one seemed like a miracle to baseball fans. After being treated with chemotherapy, Lester was back on the mound—soon becoming the first Red Sox southpaw to pitch a no-hitter in more than fifty years. After the game, Lester spoke with reporters about his ordeal in battling cancer. "It was a long road back," he told them, adding, "I'm just glad that I'm here at this moment right now."[1] The day after Kennedy was released from the hospital to return home and consider his options for treatment, he went sailing—a favorite activity.

Jon Lester celebrates after pitching a no-hitter against the Kansas City Royals on May 19, 2008. He had been diagnosed with cancer less than two years earlier.

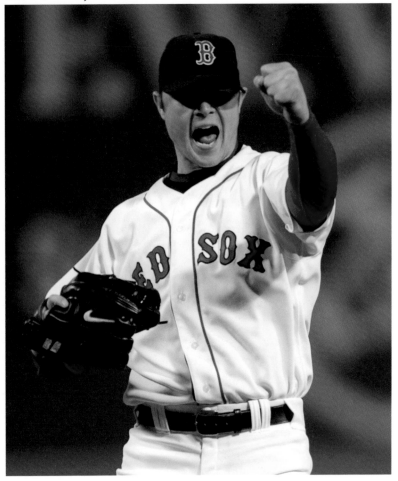

Whether they are young or old, cancer patients—like Lester and Kennedy—want to live their lives as normally as possible. People with cancer need the support of their families and friends to help them in what is often a long and painful fight, and they need to be included as much as possible in activities they enjoy.

In 1971 the United States government declared a war on cancer. Since then, billions of dollars have been spent to find new weapons to fight the disease. Many scientists have spent millions of hours trying to find better ways of treating it. Others have spent countless hours trying to find more effective ways to prevent cancer. Since the late twentieth century, tremendous progress has been made in detecting and treating cancer. Doctors and patients no longer accept a cancer diagnosis as an inevitable death sentence. In the twenty-first century, more patients are surviving cancer than ever before.

Scientists still do not know why some people get certain cancers and others do not. They do know, however, that many cancers are preventable. It has been proven that avoiding known risk factors such as tobacco smoke, excess sunlight, and some chemicals and pollutants could prevent about half the cancers that occur. A harmful lifestyle that includes poor diet, lack of exercise, and alcohol abuse may put a person at risk. As Donna Bozzone of Saint Michael's College says, "People have tremendous power to reduce their chances of developing cancer by making good health and lifestyle decisions. Even if treatments become perfect, prevention is still preferable to avoid the anxiety of a diagnosis and the potential pain of treatment."[2]

Although tremendous progress has been made in understanding cancer, it is still a mysterious disease in many ways. There are lots of myths and misconceptions about it, but doctors believe the more people are informed about the disease and its risks, the better chance they have of escaping or surviving it.

CHAPTER ONE

What Is Cancer?

Cancer is not a single disease; it is a name given to at least two hundred different diseases. Cancer occurs when normal cells in the body behave in abnormal ways. The human body consists of trillions of cells that are so tiny they can only be seen under a microscope. The organs and tissues of the body are made up of groups of these cells. All cells reproduce by dividing—a process called mitosis. Usually, when cells are no longer needed by the body for growth or repair of tissues, they die. Some cells, however, continue to divide and refuse to die when they are no longer needed.

Each cancer starts with one cell that reproduces uncontrollably. This behavior is called mutation. As the out-of-control mutant cells pile up, they form masses called tumors. When these tumors become aggressive and invasive, they are said to be malignant, or cancerous. Cancer can develop in almost any organ or tissue of the body. From its original site, a cancer may spread, or metastasize, to other parts of the body. When this happens, the cancer is more difficult to treat and may become life threatening.

Normal Cells and Cancer Cells

Normal cells and cancer cells are different in several ways. Normal cells reproduce themselves exactly and stop reproducing when they are supposed to. They self-destruct when they have completed their job or if they become damaged. Cancer cells keep on reproducing and do not obey signals to stop.

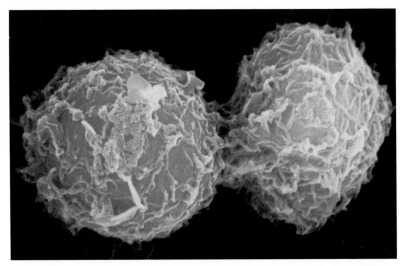

A human colon cancer cell undergoes mitosis (division). Unlike normal cells, cancer cells do not die, but continue to divide.

They have been called immortal because they refuse to die on their own. Normal cells stick together. Cancer cells do not, which allows them to become detached from their neighboring cells. Finally, normal cells mature and become specialized in doing their job. Cancer cells remain immature and even become more immature or primitive over time; they do not perform any helpful function in the body.

DNA: The Cell's Blueprint

Each cell in the human body contains long coils of deoxyribonucleic acid (DNA). Strands of DNA look like twisted strings of beads. Similar to the way letters are arranged in a sentence to provide information, the way the beads in the DNA are arranged provides information to the cells. Sections of DNA called genes are blueprints or designs for making new cells. Genes contain instructions that are passed down from generation to generation. The information in genes controls how a person will look: eye and hair color, height, and many other physical traits as well as some behavioral traits.

Genes in the DNA strand also contain complicated instructions that control the growth, division, and repair of cells.

When cells divide, each new cell gets a complete copy of all the DNA instructions from the original cell. If the original cell's genes are damaged, the damage is passed on to the new cell. The new cell can also acquire more damage, which it passes along to its offspring. When the damaged cells multiply wildly, cancer may result. Some substances that can damage cells' DNA are cigarette smoke, chemicals, radiation, and excessive sunlight. Substances that cause damage to DNA genes in such a way that cancer may occur are called carcinogens.

An illustration of a DNA helix is shown here. Genes, which are sections of DNA, are blueprints or designs for making new cells.

Oncogenes and Suppressor Genes

Some genes encourage cells to multiply. This is important in young people, who are still growing, but in adults it normally does not happen very often. Exceptions to this are after a wound or operation, when cells multiply to repair the dam-

Genetic Medicine: Blessing or Curse?

In "Genetic Medicine: Powerful Opportunities for Good and Greed," Michael Dalzell says that while genetic treatments could spawn incredible improvements in health care, they also raise complex questions. He explains:

> The theory of genetic diagnosis and treatment turns the practice of Western medicine inside out—literally. Instead of starting with disease and searching for its origin, genomics begins with a genetic variation and relies on treatments that manipulate it, often before the gene can express itself in terms of illness. It bespeaks a change in the nature of health care from treating symptoms to predicting health status and taking steps accordingly.

> Dalzell points out that while this concept fits the disease prevention goals of managed health care, it requires expensive, highly individualized treatment. Furthermore, it can be shocking to patients to know what their future is likely to hold. He asks, "At what point do you say to a 13-year-old girl: 'We've done genetic testing on you, and somewhere around age 60, you're going to develop Alzheimer's. You'll have osteoporosis by around 40. And, oh, by the way, you have an 80 percent chance of getting breast cancer'?"

Michael Dalzell, "Genetic Medicine: Powerful Opportunities for Good and Greed," *Managed Care*, May 2001, p. 4.

age. When genes become overactive and tell cells to keep on multiplying when there is no reason for it, scientists call them oncogenes, or cancer genes. These are the villains that direct cells to multiply excessively, ignoring normal stop signals. Oncogenes have been found to contribute to cancers in many places in the body, including the breasts, lungs, liver, bladder, and colon. Along with the term *oncogene* comes the name *oncologist* for a doctor who specializes in treating cancer.

Fortunately, the body normally has a way to combat these unruly oncogenes. Suppressor genes come to the rescue by limiting cell growth or division. If oncogenes are like accelerators in cars, then suppressor genes are like brakes. They stop cells with damaged genes from reproducing and encourage them to self-destruct. However, in cancerous cells, the suppressor gene may be damaged, making it unable to stop cell multiplication. One well-known suppressor gene is called p53, and in most human cancers this suppressor is damaged or missing. When genes transform into oncogenes and suppressor genes like p53 become inactive through damage, tumors may form.

Tumors

A tumor is a large group of cells that have clumped together to form a mass of tissue. Some tumors are benign. A benign tumor usually grows slowly. When it stops growing, it does not spread beyond the place where it started. Benign tumors are usually contained inside a wall or barrier called a basement membrane, which is made up of proteins (molecules of amino acids). Once a benign tumor is removed, it is not likely to form again. It is a problem only if it grows very large and becomes uncomfortable or unsightly, presses on other body organs, takes up space inside the skull, or releases hormones that cause trouble.

Malignant, or cancerous, tumors usually grow more quickly than benign tumors. They break through the basement membrane and invade surrounding tissue. They can become life threatening when cells break away and spread to other parts of the body, in a process called metastasis. There are two

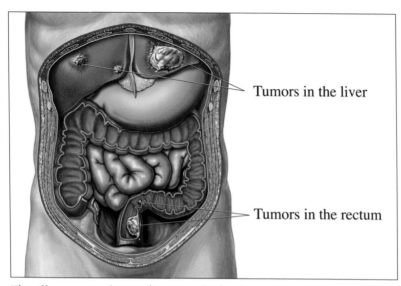

Tumors in the liver

Tumors in the rectum

This illustration shows the spread of colon cancer from the
rectum to the liver.

ways cancer cells spread through the body. They can travel
through the bloodstream to distant parts of the body. Since
the blood vessels in tumors are weaker and more leaky than
normal blood vessels, the tumor cells can escape and circulate
in the blood. Escaping tumor cells can also be carried in the
lymphatic fluid that bathes the body tissues. Then they can
establish metastatic colonies in the lymph nodes that drain all
of the tissues of the body. Once cancer cells invade another
body organ, they can grow new malignant tumors, called secondary tumors.

No matter where it spreads or how much it spreads, a cancer is always classified by the primary site where it started.
This is because wherever they are in the body, cancer cells
still possess many of the characteristics of the original tumor
cells. If a cancer starts in the breast and spreads to the lungs,
it is still classified as breast cancer. Or if a cancer starts in the
stomach and spreads to the liver, it is still classified as stomach
cancer. It is important to doctors treating the cancer to identify
the origin of the cancer so they can decide how to treat it. This
is because the organs of the body are made up of different

types of cells that behave in different ways. They may grow at different speeds and be more or less likely to spread in the blood. They also may respond differently to drugs or radiation.

How Tumor Cells Trick the Body

In order to survive, all the cells in the body need oxygen and other nutrients and a way to dispose of waste material. Blood brings these essential supplies to cells and also removes waste. This is true not only for normal body cells but also for cancerous cells in tumors. As a tumor grows bigger, the cells in its center get farther and farther from the blood vessels surrounding it. The cancer cells are in danger of starving to death unless they can develop their own blood supply. They need a clever strategy to meet this challenge, and, unfortunately, they have found it.

Normal cells stimulate new blood vessels to grow when they need to repair damaged tissue. They have genes that can switch the growth of blood vessels on and off. The formation of new blood vessels is called angiogenesis. Aggressive cancer cells send out a flood of SOS signals, by means of signaling proteins that call for more blood. New capillaries (tiny blood vessels) begin to sprout from the tissues surrounding the tumor, and tumor angiogenesis takes place. When the tumor is nourished by the new blood vessels, it begins to expand and spread. Wherever it spreads in the body, the metastatic tumor carries cells like those in the original, or primary, tumor.

Kinds of Cancers

Since there are so many different cancers, they can be classified in different ways. Most cancers, however, fit into one of three main types: carcinoma, sarcoma, and leukemia/lymphoma. About 85 to 90 percent of all cancers are carcinomas. These cancers begin in covering tissues of the body, such as the outer layer of the skin. They also occur in the delicate tissue that lines the mouth. Carcinomas may also arise in tissues lining the internal organs, the chest cavity, the abdominal cavity, and the organs of the digestive and reproductive systems.

Sarcomas originate in connective and supporting tissues, such as bones, cartilage, nerves, and fat. In addition to bone cancer, sarcomas include cancer of skeletal muscles and Kaposi's sarcoma, a skin cancer that sometimes appears in AIDS patients. Sarcomas are usually divided into two main types: bone sarcomas and soft tissue sarcomas. Together, they make up fewer than 1 percent of cancers.

Cancers of the blood cells are called leukemias. Leukemias arise in tissues where blood cells are produced, such as the bone marrow. Large numbers of abnormal white blood cells fill the bone marrow and enter the bloodstream. They interfere with the production of red blood cells and cause problems like bleeding and anemia. Leukemia is one of the most common cancers affecting children.

Lymphomas are cancers that develop in the lymphatic system. This system includes the lymph nodes, tonsils, adenoids, spleen, and bone marrow. The lymphatic system fights off germs that cause infection and illness. Lester, the Red Sox pitcher, was diagnosed and treated for a form of lymphoma called non-Hodgkin's lymphoma.

This illustration shows a carcinoma on the stomach wall. Carcinomas account for about 85 to 90 percent of all cancers.

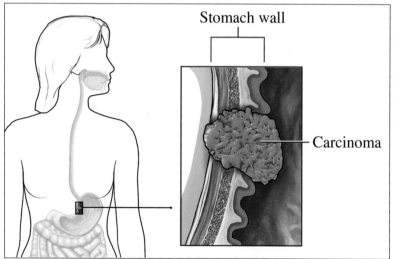

Estimated Deaths by Gender and Type of Cancer, 2008

Men

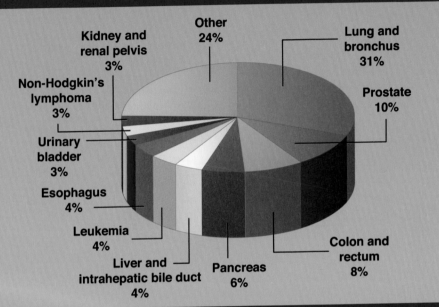

Other
24%

Kidney and renal pelvis
3%

Non-Hodgkin's lymphoma
3%

Urinary bladder
3%

Esophagus
4%

Leukemia
4%

Liver and intrahepatic bile duct
4%

Pancreas
6%

Lung and bronchus
31%

Prostate
10%

Colon and rectum
8%

Women

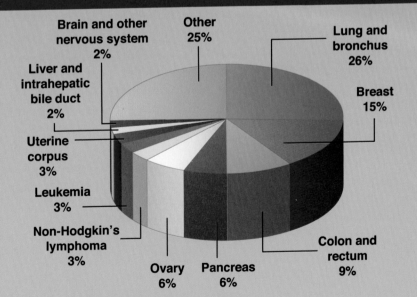

Brain and other nervous system
2%

Liver and intrahepatic bile duct
2%

Uterine corpus
3%

Leukemia
3%

Non-Hodgkin's lymphoma
3%

Ovary
6%

Pancreas
6%

Other
25%

Lung and bronchus
26%

Breast
15%

Colon and rectum
9%

Cancer Causes: Heredity or Environment?

It has been established by experts that cancers can be familial, or inherited, or sporadic, occurring at random in the population. Although most tumors arise in people with no family history of the disease, there is good reason for researchers to study both causes.

Damaged or mutated genes can be inherited. When doctors establish a patient's medical history, they ask about close relatives who have had cancer and what kind of cancer they had. Doctors know that some types of mutated genes can be passed from parents to children. They are aware that patients with a family history of certain cancers are more vulnerable to that type of cancer. But they also know that although patients with a family history of cancer are at higher risk, they are not destined to develop cancer.

Sometimes cancers that occur in several family members are just coincidental. They might also be caused by something in the shared environment. Compared to tumors that occur sporadically, the actual number of cases of familial cancer is quite small. There are, however, certain types of cancer that occur more often in families. These include some cancers of the breast, prostate cancer, ovarian cancer, cancer of the colon, skin cancers, and an eye cancer called retinoblastoma.

Genetic testing for the more common oncogenes is possible today. But this kind of testing is controversial. Although genetic tests can predict whether or not a person is at risk for certain familial cancers, many people prefer not to know. And even those who discover that they do not carry an abnormal gene mutation are still at risk for developing cancers that occur sporadically.

Those whose genetic tests indicate they have inherited an abnormal gene can choose to have more frequent tests for cancer, or they can opt for more drastic procedures. Experts have found that those who carry the breast cancer gene BRCA have an 80 percent chance of developing breast cancer. Consequently, some women who have tested positive for the BRCA gene have more frequent mammograms. Still others choose to have their

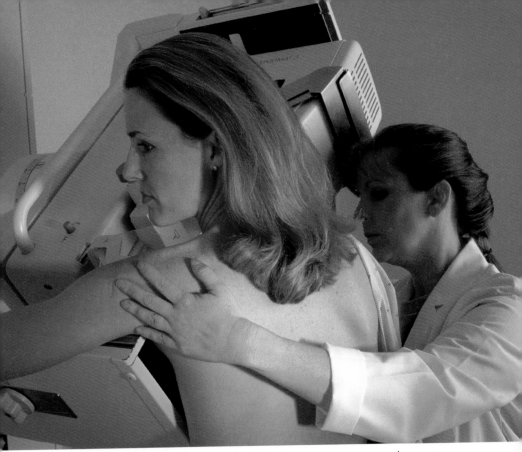

Women who are at a higher risk for breast cancer may choose to have more frequent mammograms to check for the disease.

breasts removed surgically to eliminate the risk, even if they do not have cancer.

Genetic testing can cost thousands of dollars; however, some cancer centers offer free testing in connection with research studies. Some insurance plans will pay the costs of genetic testing that is recommended by a person's doctor. But some people fear that those who have a known risk of cancer may have difficulty being hired for jobs or obtaining health or life insurance.

Carcinogens as a Cause of Cancer

Most cancers are not the result of inherited abnormal genes. They are the result of environmental factors. Some carcinogens have been known and understood for a long time. Others are being discovered through current research. The research is difficult because many cancers develop from the combined effects of more than one carcinogen on the DNA. Carcinogens enter the body through the skin or through the nose, mouth, or other openings.

Sometimes it is apparent that people who work at particular jobs tend to get certain types of cancer. Experts study chemicals or other substances these people encounter in their work. The first step is to test the suspect substance on laboratory animals such as mice or rats. If a large percentage of the animals develop cancer, the researchers go on to evaluate the effect of the substance on people. They do this by comparing a group of people who have been exposed to the agent to a group of people who have not been exposed. If the exposed group has a higher rate of a certain cancer, this is strong evidence that the substance is a carcinogen.

Asbestos is an example of a cancer-causing agent that took years to discover. Asbestos was once commonly used

Pets Get Cancer, Too

Veterinarian Karen Halligan says cancer is one of the leading causes of death in pets and accounts for nearly half of all deaths in cats and dogs over the age of ten. She says:

> Dogs suffer from more kinds of cancer (at least 100) than any other domestic animal, and one in four will develop the disease in its lifetime. Just like people, pets can develop cancer from exposure to sunlight, smoke, asbestos, chemicals, hormones, radiation and viruses, and from immune system failures. And some breeds have hereditary risk factors, among them golden retrievers, boxers and bulldogs.
>
> Like humans, pets can be treated with surgery, chemotherapy, radiation, immunotherapy, or a combination of treatments.

Karen Halligan, "How to Protect Your Pet from Cancer," *Parade*, May 11, 2008, p. 13.

A sign warns that a building contains asbestos. Asbestos is a material once commonly used in construction, but now is a known carcinogen, or cancer-causing agent.

as a building material. Workers in the construction business inhaled large amounts of asbestos fibers in the course of their work. Years later, many of them developed lung cancer. Although asbestos is no longer used in buildings, many older buildings still contain this substance. If these structures undergo renovation or are torn down and the asbestos is disturbed, the fibers float in the air and cause cancer if they are breathed in.

Through experiments, scientists have identified hundreds of chemicals that can cause cancer in animals. Some of these may also be hazardous to humans. One of the deadliest is cigarette smoke, which contains dozens of chemical carcinogens. In addition to lung cancer, smoking causes many cancers of the mouth, larynx, esophagus, pancreas, kidney, bladder, cervix, and some forms of leukemia. It can also cause cancer in non-smokers who live or work closely with smokers.

Radiation is another well-known carcinogen. It comes from different sources, but the most common source of cancer-causing radiation is the sun. Its invisible ultraviolet rays cause most cases of skin cancer, including deadly melanoma. Nuclear radiation can also cause different kinds of cancer, which sometimes do not appear until years after exposure.

At this time, experts have not determined that viruses are a major cause of human cancers. It has been shown, however, that the human papillomavirus (HPV) causes most cases of cervical cancer. Other viruses may cause cancer of the liver and adult T-cell leukemia. One of the viruses that spreads mononucleosis (commonly called the "kissing disease") is the Epstein-Barr virus (EBV). Nasopharyngeal cancer, which involves the area at the back of the nose, has been linked to EBV. There also seems to be a link with Hodgkin's disease, since people who have had EBV-related illnesses, including mono, are more likely to contract Hodgkin's disease than those who have not.

Dealing with Cancer

Cancer is a very complicated disease. It appears in many shapes and forms and has many tricks and ways of surviving. All the problems involved in preventing, diagnosing, and treating it will take many more years to solve. However, as Barbara Basler says in "Good News About Cancer": "Cancer is still a formidable foe, but in the last few years alone, scientists have gained intimate knowledge of this enemy and are using it to outmaneuver these deadly cells—prolonging life and improving cure rates for thousands of patients."[3]

CHAPTER TWO

Detecting and Treating Cancer

The earlier a cancer is detected, the better a person's chances are of a full recovery. For many cancers, early treatment can prevent the cancer from growing, invading other organs, and spreading to other parts of the body. Unfortunately, cancer is not always easy to identify, since symptoms vary greatly and may be similar to symptoms of many other illnesses. Sometimes there are no symptoms at all. Before the mid-1950s cancer was called "the silent killer." By the time they saw a doctor, most cancer patients already had advanced cancer that had spread to other parts of the body. Today, scientists are constantly finding new and better ways to detect, diagnose, and treat cancer. It is most important, however, for individuals to be aware of how they can help detect cancer at an early stage.

Cancer's Warning Signs

The American Cancer Society (ACS) recognizes seven warning signs that may indicate cancer:

Change in bowel or bladder habits
A sore that does not go away
Unusual bleeding or discharge
Thickening or lump in neck, breast, or other area
Indigestion or difficulty swallowing
Obvious change in wart or mole
Nagging cough or hoarseness

The first letters of the seven signs spell "caution." People who note one or more of these signs may not have cancer, but they should report their symptoms to their doctor. Another suspicious symptom is unusual tiredness, especially when it is combined with one of the seven signs listed by the ACS.

The ABCDE Rule

Melanoma, the most serious kind of skin cancer, is a widespread type of cancer in the United States. Physicians say it is important that everyone keep a careful watch for any changes in moles on their bodies, as these could be signs of melanoma. Doctors recommend checking moles using the ABCDE rule:

A for asymmetry
A mole that does not look the same on both sides.

B for border
A mole with edges that are ragged or fuzzy.

C for color
A mole that varies in shade from dark brown to red or blue or that has lost color.

D for difference
A mole that has changed in size, shape, or color or become itchy.

E for elevation
A mole that is raised above the skin and has an uneven surface.

If any of these symptoms exist, it is recommended that the individual schedule a checkup with a dermatologist.

An unexplained drop in energy, combined with any of the seven warning signs identified by the American Cancer Society, may indicate the presence of cancer.

Clark played football in high school and was a frequent basketball and tennis player all through his four years of college. He appeared to have boundless energy. He was president of his fraternity. He drove a school bus for several hours a day to earn extra spending money. He could study into the early hours for an exam and ace it the next day. When he entered medical school, he developed a hacking cough that wouldn't go away. He also began losing weight. Because his parents lived in a town some distance away, he was able to keep them from knowing what was going on. At this exciting point in his life he did not want any interruptions!

When his energy began to lag and the nagging cough continued, his girlfriend urged him to see a doctor. But Clark was too busy trying to keep up with classwork and the lab experiments he was doing in connection with mice and cancer drugs. Finally, though, when he developed night sweats and could barely drag himself through the day, he went to the school's doctor. Tests revealed he had Hodgkin's disease, a malignant disease of the lymphatic system. Clark's cancer was extensive, and he underwent a series of chemotherapy treatments. The treatments left him nauseated and fatigued, and they caused his hair to fall out. He had to drop all of his classes except two. In those two he did well, making As.

After months of treatment, Clark's cancer went into remission. His hair grew back, and he got back some of his old energy and drive. Unfortunately, within a few months the cancer returned, and Clark had to undergo another round of chemotherapy. He is again slowly recovering and hopes to be able to resume his medical studies. He and his family and friends often wonder, though, what would have happened if he had paid attention to the early warning signs.

Self-Examination for Men and Women

Early cancer usually does not cause pain. Even when warning symptoms—like those experienced by Clark—develop, many people do not check with their doctors. They know the same symptoms can occur with illnesses other than cancer. It is not easy to face the possibility of cancer, so they ignore the warnings. This can be a big mistake.

In addition to paying attention to warning symptoms, everyone needs to practice self-exams regularly. Women should do monthly breast self-examinations, following the instructions of their doctor or other health-care provider. They should be alert for lumps, knots, thickening, or dimpling in their breasts and for any changes in the appearance of the nipples. These changes should be reported to their doctor. Although most breast lumps are not cancer, only a professional examiner can make a diagnosis.

Men should do monthly testicular self-exams, checking for lumps, swelling, and tenderness or pain in their testicles. Testicular cancer occurs most often in men between the ages of fifteen and forty. In *Cancer Information for Teens*, Wilma R. Caldwell writes: "For men, starting at age 15, monthly self-exams of the testicles are an effective way of detecting testicular cancer at an early—and very curable—stage."[4] In addition to lumps, swelling, or enlargement in the testicle, warning signs of testicular cancer may include an ache in the lower abdomen, back, or groin, or pain in the testicle or the scrotum.

Lance Armstrong is perhaps the best-known survivor of testicular cancer. The cycling champion has won multiple international contests, and has been called the best cyclist ever. In 1996, when the twenty-five-year-old athlete began having severe pain in his groin, he went to see a doctor. He was diagnosed with testicular cancer, which had spread to his lungs, stomach, and brain. After a long period of difficult treatments, he returned to successful competition.

Thirty-nine-year-old world and Olympic figure-skating champion Scott Hamilton's warning symptom was a persistent stomachache. In 1997 Hamilton's doctor discovered that his problem was testicular cancer. The overall cure rate for this type of cancer is over 90 percent when it is detected early, and Hamilton appears to be one of the lucky ones.

Looking for Subtle Signs

Armstrong and Hamilton were fortunate that warning symptoms made them check with their doctors. Sometimes the signs are subtle or vague—or missing entirely, until it is too late for successful treatment. Everyone should be aware of what is going on with their own bodies by giving themselves regular checkups—at least in the areas that can be seen or felt.

Oral cancers can affect all areas of the mouth, including the lips, the teeth, the tongue, the gums, the lining of the cheeks, the floor of the mouth, and the bony top of the mouth. Self-examination is done by looking in a mirror to check for changes in the color of the lips, gums, tongue, or inner cheek and to search for scabs, cracks, sores, white patches, swelling, or bleeding. Any abnormalities should be reported to a doctor.

Basal cell carcinoma of the skin is the most common human cancer. It arises from the basal cells—small, round cells found in the outer layer of the skin. Squamous cell carcinoma of the skin begins in the thin, flat cells resembling fish scales found in

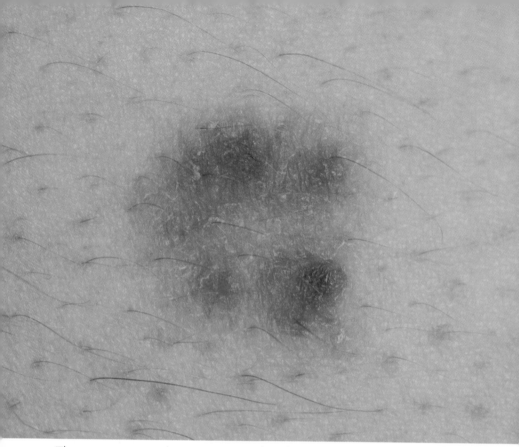

The most common human cancer is basal cell carcinoma of the skin.

the tissue that forms the surface of the skin. Melanoma arises in the cells that produce pigment and usually begins in a mole. Common signs that warn of skin cancer or the potential of skin cancer are spots on the skin that grow and do not heal; bleeding sores that will not go away; and moles that keep growing, are itchy, or change shape or color.

Screening Tests for Cancer

Many people are alive today because they observed the warning signs of cancer or discovered suspicious areas through self-examination and reported these to their doctors. Others are alive because of cancer-screening procedures that are practiced routinely in many countries. Screening for cancer across a healthy population can identify individuals who have the disease but do not as yet have symptoms—in other words, looking for cancer before it shows any signs. The World Health

Organization says successful screening programs depend on three principles:

- The target disease should be a common form of cancer, with high associated morbidity [sickness] and mortality [death].
- Effective treatment, capable of reducing morbidity and mortality, should be available.
- Test procedures should be acceptable, safe, and relatively inexpensive.[5]

Some proven screening tests have undoubtedly saved many lives. Mammograms are low-dose X-rays of the breasts that can reveal tumors. The Pap test is used to screen for cervical cancer. In this test, a doctor scrapes sample cells from the cervix, which is located at the top of the vagina. The cells are then checked by microscopic examination for cancer or changes that may lead to cancer. In older men, prostate cancer is common, and there are several effective screening tests for this type of cancer. There are also several methods of screening for colon cancer.

Diagnosing Cancer

When routine screening tests or signs or symptoms indicate that cancer may be present, a doctor will usually order various tests. Laboratory examination of blood and urine samples may yield important information. There are also ways doctors can actually look inside the body. Tests that make pictures of the inside of the body are known as imaging tests.

X-rays are the most common imaging test. As X-rays pass through the body, they create images that are recorded on special photographic film. Since X-rays pass through soft tissue more easily than dense tissue, solid tumors show up against the softer tissue around them.

Computerized axial tomography, also known as CAT scans, produces clearer, more detailed pictures than ordinary X-ray images. The CAT scan sends tiny streams of X-rays through the body at various angles. Although a CAT scan cannot detect

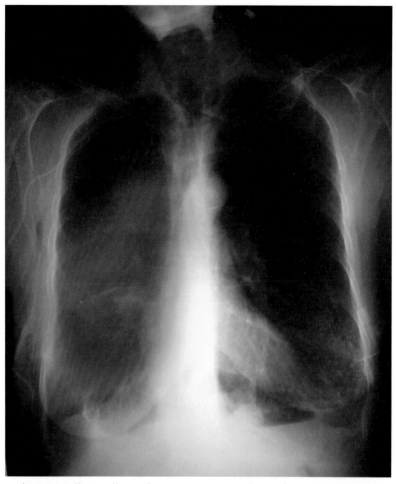

A doctor will usually order various tests if signs or symptoms indicate that cancer may be present in a patient. An X-ray is a common imaging test. This X-ray shows the presence of lung cancer.

very small tumors, it can detect tumors in internal organs, such as the lungs and brain, and can provide valuable information about a tumor's size and type.

Magnetic resonance imaging, or MRI, is more sophisticated than a CAT scan. It uses a powerful magnet linked to a computer to make detailed pictures of different areas in the body. These pictures can be viewed on a monitor and can also be printed out.

Even more efficient and specialized imaging tests are constantly being devised to detect the most elusive cancers.

Biopsy

After a tumor is discovered, the next step is to determine whether it is benign or malignant. The only sure way to know is through a biopsy. In a biopsy, a sample of tissue is taken from the abnormal area, or the whole tumor may be removed. The sample is examined under a microscope to determine whether it is malignant and, if so, what kind of cancer it is and whether the cells are likely to grow rapidly or slowly.

One method of obtaining material in a biopsy is by using an endoscope—a long fiber-optic cable with a small forceps on the end. The endoscope can be inserted into internal body cavities such as the bronchus, trachea, bladder, or gastrointestinal tract. The doctor can then view the area and may use the forceps to remove a tissue sample from a suspicious region.

A biopsy is used to determine whether a tumor is benign or malignant. Pictured here is a close-up of a brain tumor removed during a biopsy.

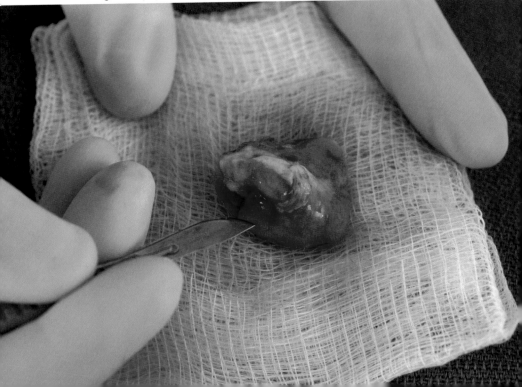

In other areas of the body biopsies are performed by fine needle aspiration. This procedure involves pushing a small, hollow needle into the suspicious area and removing a sample of cells to analyze. Fine needle aspiration is particularly useful for reaching suspicious areas that would be difficult to reach without doing major surgery. Biopsies of the breasts, thyroid gland, pancreas, lungs, and liver are usually done this way. Leukemia patients may undergo a bone marrow biopsy in which a needle is inserted into the marrow cavity of a bone and a portion of the bone marrow is removed for examination. If the tests on the biopsied cells come back positive, the patient can begin treatment quickly, increasing the chance for a full recovery. Treatment is aimed at removing or killing cancer cells.

Treating Cancer

Oncologists today have a number of different options in treating cancer patients. Sometimes they use a combination of methods. For example, after surgery is used to remove the main tumor mass, chemotherapy and/or radiation treatment may be used to kill any stray cancer cells that have escaped from the tumor. The kind of treatment recommended will depend on the patient's age, health, and medical history as well as on the type of cancer, how much it has grown, and whether or not it has spread from its original location.

Surgery

Surgery is the oldest type of cancer treatment, and it is still the first and best option for many tumors in the earliest stages. If the tumor can be removed before it has metastasized, the patient can be completely cured. In conventional surgery, the surgeon must try to cut out all of the cancer cells, even if it means taking out some normal tissue surrounding the tumor. In addition to cutting out the tumor, the surgeon may remove one or more of the nearby lymph nodes. If the lymph nodes contain tumor cells, that means the cancer has spread beyond the site of its origin and may already have migrated to other tissues. If the nodes are positive for cancer cells, additional therapy, such as chemotherapy, is likely to be indicated.

Cryosurgery, also called cryotherapy, is a technique of freezing and killing abnormal cells. It can be used on both internal tumors and external tumors such as those on the skin. In cryosurgery, liquid nitrogen or argon gas is used to produce extreme cold. For skin tumors, liquid nitrogen is applied directly to the cancer with a swab or spraying device. For internal tumors, liquid nitrogen or argon gas is circulated through a hollow instrument called a cryoprobe, which is placed in contact with the tumor. Although cryosurgery is not appropriate for all cancers, it has some important advantages over conventional surgery. It has fewer side effects, it is less expensive, and it requires a shorter recovery time.

Laser surgery is a technique in which the surgeon uses a focused beam of high-energy light to vaporize cancer cells. In this high-tech method of zapping tumors, surrounding tissue is not destroyed. The laser produces heat that sterilizes the surgical site, so there is a lower risk of infection. Today, laser surgery is the standard treatment for a number of kinds of cancer.

Chemotherapy

Chemotherapy—treatment with powerful chemicals—has proven to be an effective method of fighting cancer. Chemotherapy can be given in different ways: through a vein (intravenously, or IV), orally, using an injection or shot, or by applying directly to the skin. When the drugs are given by mouth, they are in the form of pills, capsules, or liquid. Needles and syringes are used to give injections either into a muscle, under the skin, or directly into cancerous areas in the skin. The drugs may also be applied to the surface of the skin. But most often chemotherapy is given intravenously.

The side effects of chemotherapy vary with each individual. The drugs used in chemotherapy are often very toxic. Common side effects are nausea, fatigue, weight loss, and hair loss. Donna, a young college professor, underwent chemotherapy after having a cancerous breast removed. The cancer had metastasized, and the potent drugs used in the chemo treatment were designed to find and destroy cells that had spread. Donna kept on with her teaching schedule. She explained her condition to her students so they understood why she was

A female cancer patient receives chemotherapy. Chemotherapy is an effective method of fighting cancer.

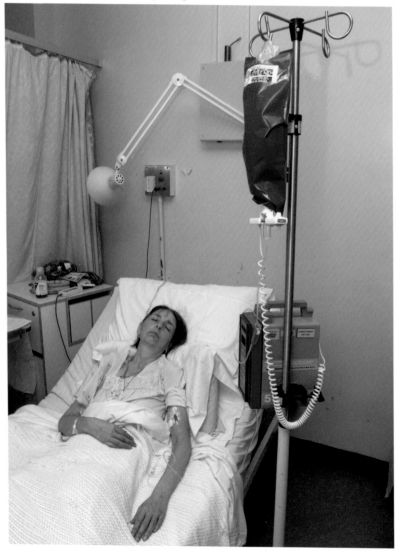

often so tired she remained seated during classes. They also understood that the brightly colored bandannas she wore covered her hair loss. Their sympathetic understanding enabled her to keep teaching—a job she loved and one that kept her from brooding over her condition. Other cancer patients, like Clark, manage to keep up with their careers by cutting down on their workload.

Radiation

Radiation therapy is another common way to treat cancer. According to the National Cancer Institute, more than half of all patients with cancer undergo some form of radiation therapy during treatment. Radiation may be used alone or in combination with other types of treatment. Different kinds of cancer are treated with different types of radiation. Sometimes the goal of radiation is to completely destroy a tumor. In other cases, the goal is to shrink a tumor and relieve symptoms such as pain.

In external radiation therapy, a special machine outside the body delivers X-rays to tumors inside the body. To help protect normal cells from the effects of radiation, the treatments are usually given in small doses five days a week for a period of several weeks. The treatments are painless.

Internal radiation, in which small capsules or other vessels containing the radiation are implanted into or near a tumor, is less commonly used. This procedure may require a hospital stay of a few days. Other ways of delivering internal radiation are to have the patient swallow a radioactive material or to inject a radioactive substance into the bloodstream or body cavity.

Some radiation patients suffer no side effects from the treatment. For those who do, the most common side effects are fatigue and skin irritation. Depending on the type of cancer and its location in the body, radiation treatment may cause patients to suffer from diarrhea, hair loss, and dental problems. Fortunately for most people, the side effects disappear in a few months after the treatments are over.

Feeling Better by Looking Better

In addition to the trauma of having the disease, cancer patients have to cope with various side effects brought on by treatments. For example, hair loss is a major concern for chemotherapy patients. There are a number of nonprofit organizations, though, that help cancer patients feel better about their appearance. Locks of Love and Wigs for Kids were created to provide complimentary hairpieces for children and young adults undergoing chemotherapy. People can donate their long hair to these organizations, which then make the hair into custom-made wigs for eligible patients.

Look Good . . . Feel Better is a program developed by the Personal Care Products Council Foundation in cooperation with the American Cancer Society. At the local level, beauticians from various salons donate their time and talent to hold workshops at which they instruct cancer patients in skin care, makeup, and the use of wigs, turbans, and scarves to help them look better. Large cosmetic companies donate generous gifts of makeup and perfumes, which the beauticians distribute to participants. There is also a Look Good . . . Feel Better for Teens, which offers an Internet network as well as local meetings.

Other Cancer Treatments

Researchers are constantly searching for better ways to treat cancer. Some of their discoveries have proven to be lifesavers. For example, leukemia was once considered incurable. Today bone marrow transplants give hope to thousands of leukemia victims.

Immunotherapy works to use the body's own defense system to fight cancer. It uses substances designed to strengthen the patient's immune system and make it more effective in recognizing and attacking cancer cells. Vaccines are also used to stimulate the immune system. Interferons, chemical messengers used to fight viruses, inhibit tumor cells from reproducing. Hormonal treatments are also under study. Hormones are substances secreted by certain glands that pass into the blood and stimulate the action of specific organs. It has been shown that certain hormones made by the testes and ovaries can influence the growth of tumors in the breast and prostate. Today, instead of surgically removing the testes or ovaries, drugs are used to block the effects of these hormones.

Although there are other new and potentially helpful treatments being studied by researchers, in general, doctors and cancer treatment facilities do not accept alternative treatments. These treatments include special diets, medicines made from various plants, and vitamin supplements. The National Cancer Institute is constantly reviewing and testing alternative treatments to weigh their possible benefits against the possibility of their doing harm. Most doctors agree that trying to cure cancer with alternative therapies alone may keep patients from receiving standard treatments that have been proven effective.

CHAPTER THREE

Preventing Cancer

Preventing cancer is much better than trying to find ways to treat it after it has occurred. Cancer prevention has much to do with identifying and avoiding risk factors that may trigger the disease. Most cancers take a long time to develop, and the way people take care of their bodies may help determine their susceptibility to cancer. However, experts do not agree about many supposed risks for cancer, leaving many people unsure of what to avoid and what precautions to take. Still, educating oneself about proven risks is a necessary strategy if one is to avoid or overcome the disease.

Control of Risk Factors

Some cancer risk factors cannot be controlled. Age—the single most important risk factor for cancer—is one over which people have no control. More than half of all cancers occur in older people. The other risk factor beyond human control is heredity. People cannot choose the genes they inherit. Although cancer caused by inherited genes is infrequent, if a certain type of cancer has occurred in close relatives, a person may opt to have more frequent screenings or to undergo genetic tests. But beyond these two uncontrollable risk factors, most proven risk factors can be avoided or controlled.

Tobacco

In 1982 the surgeon general of the United States reported that cigarette smoking was the major cause of cancer deaths in the country. This statement is still true. Experts estimate that one-third of all cancer deaths are caused by the use of tobacco. The American Cancer Society reports that most lung cancer deaths are caused by smoking. Smoking is also a major cause of cancers of the larynx, throat, oral cavity, esophagus, and bladder. It also contributes to the development of cancers of the pancreas, cervix, kidney, stomach, and some leukemias.

Cigarette smoke contains dozens of chemical carcinogens, and it can harm nearly every organ in the body. In addition to cancer, it causes heart disease and other serious illnesses. Smoking costs billions of dollars in health care each year. It is the most avoidable environmental cause of cancer, yet Americans still light up. Every two years the federal government conducts a Youth Risk Behavior Survey of students in grades nine through twelve. The survey tracks a variety of risk behaviors, including drug, alcohol, and tobacco use. In June 2008 the results of the latest survey showed that one out of every five students in the survey smoked cigarettes regularly.

Experts agree that choosing "light," "low-tar," or "mild" cigarettes does not reduce the health risk associated with smoking.

States with the Highest Percentage of Smokers, 2006

State	Percentage (%) of Population
Kentucky	28.6
West Virginia	25.7
Oklahoma	25.1
Mississippi	25.1
Alaska	24.2
Indiana	24.1
Arkansas	23.7
Louisiana	23.4
Alabama	23.3
Missouri	23.3

Taken from: American Cancer Society. Available online at: http://www.cancer.org/downloads/STT/CPED_2008.pdf.

When Smoking Was In

Until late in the twentieth century, cigarette smoking was more in the public eye. In the early days of TV, many newscasters used cigarettes as sophisticated props. There were clever ads for smoking on TV, and magazines were filled with colorful full-page ads for different brands of cigarettes. Cigarette companies even advertised in medical journals. During World War II, the government regularly issued cigarettes to everyone in the armed forces. In movies, leading characters often smoked, making the habit seem glamorous to viewers.

Today, the trend has been reversed. Laws have banned cigarette advertising on billboards and in public venues frequented by children. Several states have antismoking laws in restaurants, malls, and other public places. On television, smoking has been banned since 1971, but it persists in movies. In July 2008, however, six major studios announced plans to include antismoking announcements on millions of DVDs of motion pictures that include smoking. The main force behind these bans and announcements has been the U.S. surgeon general's persistent warning that smoking is linked to several ailments, including cancer. The surgeon general first made this public pronouncement in 1964, and, overnight, smoking became less a matter of personal choice than an issue of public health.

There is no such thing as a safe cigarette. Cigar smoking is also associated with cancers of the lip, tongue, mouth, and throat as well as of the lung. Like cigarette smokers, cigar smokers who start early in life and smoke most often are at the greatest risk.

Chewing tobacco contains twenty-eight carcinogens. It is sometimes called "spitting" tobacco because people spit out the tobacco juices that combine with saliva and build up in their mouths. In 1986 the surgeon general concluded that the use of smokeless tobacco "is not a safe substitute for smoking cigarettes. It can cause cancer and a number of noncancerous conditions and can lead to nicotine addiction and dependence."[6]

Secondhand Smoke

A person does not have to be a smoker to be at risk for harm caused by tobacco smoke. Secondhand smoke is smoke released from the end of a lit cigarette or cigar or smoke exhaled by a smoker. Nonsmokers who are exposed to secondhand smoke absorb nicotine and other toxic chemicals just

Despite evidence demonstrating the connection between smoking and cancer, teenagers are still smoking.

as smokers do. The U.S. Environmental Protection Agency (EPA) and the International Agency for Research on Cancer (a branch of the World Health Organization) have classified secondhand smoke as a "known human carcinogen."[7]

The 2006 U.S. surgeon general's report reached the conclusion that secondhand smoke causes lung cancer and that there is no safe level of exposure to secondhand smoke. The report said that ventilating buildings and separating smokers from nonsmokers is not enough to protect nonsmokers. It recommended banning all smoking in buildings and spaces where smokers and nonsmokers are together.

Children are especially sensitive to secondhand smoke. Even if they don't live in a home with a regular smoker, they can be exposed to secondhand smoke in public places such as shopping centers, public transportation, and restaurants. For adults, the workplace is a major source of secondhand smoke exposure. Today, more and more nations are enacting clean indoor air laws to protect people from secondhand smoke.

Ultraviolet (UV) Rays

Skin cancer is the most common of all types of cancer. Most skin cancers are caused by exposure to too much ultraviolet (UV) radiation from the sun or tanning beds.

It is estimated that more than 1 million new cases of skin cancer occur each year. In recent decades, the rates of all kinds of skin cancers have been increasing. Certain people are more susceptible to skin cancer. This high-risk group includes those who work outside, like to sunbathe, use a tanning bed, have a family history of skin cancer, are fair skinned, or have a lot of moles.

Basal and squamous cell skin cancers are the most common varieties. They are also referred to as non-melanoma skin cancers to differentiate them from the more deadly form of skin cancer called melanoma. Basal and squamous cell skin cancers appear mainly on parts of the body exposed to the sun. They seldom spread, but if left untreated they can grow quite large and invade and destroy nearby tissues.

People can reduce the risk of developing skin cancer by using sunscreen when they plan on being in the sun.

Melanoma is responsible for 77 percent of all skin cancer deaths, but if it is caught and treated early, the cure rate is about 95 percent. Melanoma can spread to major organs such as the lungs, the liver, and the brain. For 2008 the National Cancer Institute estimated a total of more than sixty-two thousand new cases of melanoma in the United States and more than eight thousand deaths from it. Many of those deaths could be prevented if everyone were aware of the warning signs of skin cancer and took precautions to protect their skin cells from damage by excessive UV rays.

Three important warning signs people should watch for are:
• Spots that grow in size and do not heal
• Moles that grow, itch, or change shape or color
• Bleeding sores that do not go away

Commonsense preventive measures include:
• Limiting exposure to the sun between 10 A.M. and 4 P.M.
• Wearing broad-brimmed hats while outdoors in the sun

- Wearing tightly woven protective clothing while outdoors in the sun
- Using a waterproof sunscreen with a sun protection factor (SPF) of 15 or higher
- Staying out of tanning beds
- Having a doctor check any suspicious-looking skin lesions

Radon Gas

Radon, an invisible, odorless gas, is the leading cause of lung cancer among nonsmokers in America. The Environmental Protection Agency says it claims about twenty-one thousand lives annually. Radon, which is produced from the natural decay of uranium, is found in nearly all soils. Radon moves up through the ground to the air above and into houses through

Dangerous Research

Working as a team in France, Pierre and Marie Curie were husband-and-wife scientists who spent much of their lives investigating radiations given off by radioactive substances. From tons of uranium ore, they isolated small amounts of two highly radioactive new chemical elements, naming them radium and polonium. In 1903 they were awarded the Nobel Prize in Physics for their work. When Pierre died suddenly in an accident three years later, Marie carried on with their research. In 1911 she received the Nobel Prize in Chemistry.

During World War I, Marie, with the help of her daughter Irene, worked on X-rays for medical diagnosis in the treatment of wounded soldiers. After the war, Marie continued her research in radiation therapy, for which she won international acclaim. When she became ill with leukemia and died, Irene and her husband carried on with the work. Like her mother, Irene became ill with leukemia and died from it in 1956 in the Curie Hospital in Paris.

cracks and holes in the foundations. The house then traps radon inside. Over time, the radon can accumulate to high levels.

The EPA estimates that about one in every fifteen homes in the United States has dangerous radon levels. Kristy Miller, spokeswoman for the EPA's Office of Radiation and Indoor Air says, "You can't touch it, you can't feel it. It is an inert gas. It's in your home for a long time, leaving no trail of evidence. It's only your proactive interest and testing that's going to prevent this health risk."[8]

Relatively inexpensive radon test kits are sold at hardware stores, and some local health departments sell them at cost to homeowners. If high levels of radon are discovered, a radon contractor can be hired to fix the problem. Some states require radon testing be done before a home can be sold, and some new homes are being built to be radon resistant.

Nuclear Radiation

Nuclear radiation has caused thousands of cancer deaths. In World War II, when atomic bombs were dropped on the Japanese cities of Hiroshima and Nagasaki, the bombs released huge amounts of nuclear radiation. Among those who survived the explosions, many were diagnosed with leukemia in the following years. There was a 50 percent increase in the number of leukemia cases in Japan from 1946 to the early 1950s.

Sadako Sasaki was two years old when the atomic bomb exploded over her home in Hiroshima. She survived to become a runner who won many races at her school. When she was eleven, shortly after winning an important race, she was diagnosed with leukemia. On October 26, 1955, a small article in the Hiroshima newspaper briefly reported her death. It said, "The death of Sadako Sasaki is the fourteenth death in Noboricho Junior High School this year. She had been sick since last fall with the atomic bomb disease. She was exposed to the atomic bomb ten years ago, and now she is gone . . . fourteenth death in this school . . . seventh grader . . . age twelve."[9]

The enthusiasm for nuclear power plants as a source of energy has been dampened by fear of accidents at the plants,

The nuclear reactor meltdown at Chernobyl released radioactive material into the air that caused a sharp increase in cancer rates in eastern Europe.

which can lead to deaths from cancer caused by radiation. In March 1979 the nuclear reactor at Three Mile Island in Pennsylvania experienced a major accident. To prevent a disastrous meltdown, radioactive air was pumped into the atmosphere. Conservative estimates put the number of people who died from leukemia and other cancers because of exposure to the toxic air at more than three hundred. Cleaning up the plant took more than six years and cost $1 billion.

In April 1986 there was an even more horrendous accident at the Chernobyl nuclear power plant in the Soviet Union. A reactor melted down, spewing radioactive materials over a wide area. Whole communities around Chernobyl were devastated, and the soil was so contaminated that crops could no longer be grown there. In addition to the people who were killed or injured in the accident, numerous cancer deaths have occurred over the years from the radiation. Scientists on the International Commission on Radiological Protection have said that the exact number of radiation-related cancers resulting from the Chernobyl disaster will never be known. They have, however, estimated that at least nine thousand fatal radiation-induced cancers resulted from this disaster. The accidents at Three Mile Island and Chernobyl have resulted in a greater understanding of the cancer risk of radiation and a tighter control of nuclear power.

Industrial Chemicals

People who are constantly exposed to carcinogens in their workplaces are at an increased risk for cancer. The more frequent the exposure and the higher the level of exposure, the greater the risk. Manufacturers and farmers who handle fertilizers and pesticides may be at risk. Truck drivers and tollbooth workers on busy highways are exposed to high levels of diesel exhaust. People who work as dry cleaners or furniture finishers handle solvents and other materials that are carcinogenic. So do people who work in laboratories and chemical factories.

Many known carcinogens used in industries have been banned by the government, like asbestos, or regulated, like benzene, nickel, and petroleum. Federal, state, and local governments also protect public health by regulating emissions of hazardous materials that pass into air, water, and land during the manufacturing process.

Viruses

During the past two decades scientists have demonstrated that viruses do cause some cancers. Experts estimate that viruses cause about 5 percent of cancer deaths in the United States today. Certain viruses can damage the DNA and then kill the host cell, increasing the risk of cancer.

The common wart-causing human papillomavirus has been linked to many cases of cervical cancer. Other papillomaviruses are linked to skin cancer. Hepatitis B and C viruses are associated with deadly liver cancer, sometimes many years after the patient has been infected with either one. The human T-cell leu-

A child suffers from Burkitt's lymphoma. Burkitt's lymphoma has been linked to the Epstein-Barr virus, which is a herpes virus that causes mononucleosis.

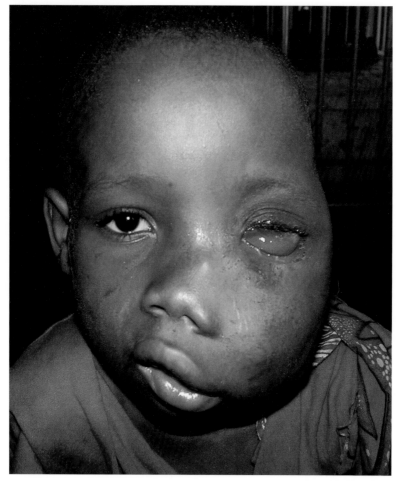

kemia/lymphoma virus (HTLV) damages white blood cells called T cells and causes leukemia in adults. Cases of leukemia caused by this virus have been reported in the southeastern United States as well as in Japan, Africa, Italy, and South America.

The Epstein-Barr virus, a herpes virus that causes mononucleosis, has been linked to Burkitt's lymphoma, which is found mainly in children in Africa. It is also associated with Hodgkin's disease, which occurs most often in adolescents and young adults. The human immunodeficiency virus (HIV), well known as the cause of AIDS, is linked with non-Hodgkin's lymphoma and Kaposi's sarcoma.

Ways to prevent infections caused by these dangerous viruses are still being studied, and the concept that viruses can cause cancer is fairly new. With viruses that are sexually transmitted, like HIV and hepatitis, practicing safe sex is a good precaution. And washing hands carefully and not touching the mouth and nose is a good way to avoid germs of all kinds.

Vaccines

The use of vaccines is a preventive measure under extensive study. There are two types of cancer vaccines. One is intended to treat existing cancers, and the other is intended to prevent cancers from developing. As of mid-2008, the United States Food and Drug Administration (FDA) has licensed two vaccines to prevent viruses that can lead to cancer.

The hepatitis B virus (HBV) causes a serious disease that affects the liver. It can cause an acute short-term illness, which in some people may go on to cause a chronic long-term infection. Chronic HBV infection can be very serious indeed, leading to liver cancer and death. The Department of Health and Human Services estimates that 1.25 million people in the United States have chronic HBV infection. The department reports that a vaccine can prevent hepatitis B and the serious consequences of HBV infection, including liver cancer. Since routine hepatitis B vaccination of U.S. children began in 1991, the reported incidence of acute hepatitis B among children and adolescents has dropped by more than 95 percent.

In June 2006 the Advisory Committee on Immunization Practices (ACIP) voted to recommend Gardasil, the first vaccine developed to prevent cervical cancer (and other diseases) caused by some types of human papillomavirus. It is recommended for eleven- to twelve-year-old girls and can be given to girls as young as nine. The vaccine is recommended for young girls because ideally it should be administered before one becomes sexually active. The vaccine is given in a series of three shots over a six-month period. Studies have shown that the vaccine provides protection for at least five years, and further studies are being done to see if a booster vaccine is needed later on.

Diet and Cancer

News stories on television and in magazines and newspapers often report studies that indicate certain foods should or should not be eaten to prevent cancer. However, the American Cancer Society advises that it is not a good idea to change one's diet based on a single study or news report. The ACS has made its own studies and come up with guidelines about avoiding cancer risk factors through what people eat and drink.

With regard to drinking alcohol, the ACS reports:

Alcohol raises the risk of cancers of the mouth, pharynx (throat), larynx (voice box), esophagus, liver, and breast, and probably of the colon and rectum. People who drink alcohol should limit their intake to no more than 2 drinks per day for men and 1 drink per day for women. A drink is defined as 12 ounces of beer, 5 ounces of wine, or 1.5 ounces of 80-proof distilled spirits. The combination of alcohol and tobacco increases the risk of some cancers far more than the effect of either drinking or smoking alone.[10]

Metabolism is the name given to the chemical changes that are continuously going on in the body's cells. Damage to tissues in the body happens constantly as a result of oxidation (normal metabolism). Antioxidant nutrients (such as vitamins A, C, and E, and beta-carotene) neutralize potential cell damage caused by oxidation. Common fruits and vegetables contain lots of antioxidants and phytochemicals (plant-based chemicals), which have been shown to lower the risk of cancer. Clinical studies have not shown that taking vitamin or mineral supplements works in the same way as eating fruits and vegetables does. In fact, the studies show that some high-dose supplements may actually increase cancer risk. The best advice from medical experts remains to eat at least five servings of fruit and vegetables every day. So far, no research exists to demonstrate whether food labeled "organic" (grown without pesticides and genetic modification) is more effective in reducing cancer risk than the same foods produced by standard methods.

Hot dogs are known to contain nitrites, which can react with the body's chemicals and change into carcinogens.

Benefits of a Plant-Based Diet

American Cancer Society guidelines say, "Research studies have found that people who routinely eat large amounts of fruits and vegetables are half as likely to develop cancer as people who don't. The foods within a plant-based diet, mostly fruits and vegetables, contain a variety of nutrients and phytochemicals—fiber and plant chemicals that protect against cancer and other diseases."

Quoted in "Eat Well, Live Longer," *OncoLog* 52, no. 1 (January 2007).

Hot dogs and most lunch meats contain nitrites, which are chemical additives used to preserve and add flavoring. Nitrites can react with chemicals in the body and change into carcinogens. Americans eat more than 20 billion hot dogs each year. A study conducted at the University of Southern California reported that eating large quantities of hot dogs might cause leukemia in children. Today, vitamin C is added to nitrite-containing meats to counteract the carcinogenic effects of nitrites.

Nutritionists say that meat should be cooked well enough to kill harmful germs. Some research, however, suggests that frying, broiling, or grilling meats at very high temperatures forms chemicals that might increase the risk of cancer. Eating excessive amounts of fat, leading to obesity, has also been linked with cancers of the breast, colon, rectum, pancreas, prostate, gall bladder, ovaries, and uterus.

Exercise and Cancer

In addition to the research currently under way to discover exactly how diet contributes to preventing cancer, studies are being done to determine the effects of being overweight and a lack of physical activity on cancer risk. In February 2001 a panel of experts met at the International Agency for Research on Cancer in Lyon, France, and concluded that being overweight and leading a sedentary lifestyle are associated with an increased risk of cancer.

The panel recommended that prevention of obesity, based on healthy eating habits and regular exercise, should begin early in life. Many studies have shown that American children are becoming increasingly obese at an alarming rate. Spending long hours sitting in front of TVs or computers and consuming lots of fried and fatty foods are major contributing factors. The ACS says: "Each year, about 550,000 Americans die of cancer; fully one-third of these deaths are linked to poor diet, physical inactivity, and carrying excess weight. Being overweight works in a variety of ways to increase cancer risk. One of the main ways is that excess weight causes the body to produce and circulate more of the hormones estrogen and insulin, which can stimulate cancer growth."[11]

A man measures himself with a tape measure. Cancer researchers have drawn a connection between cancer and obesity.

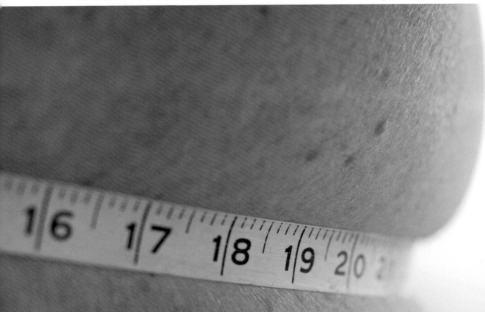

The Sunshine Vitamin

Although too much sun can increase the risk of getting skin cancer, studies show that a limited amount of sun exposure can cut the risk of getting other cancers. A team of researchers at the University of California, San Diego, reports that a daily intake of 1,000 international units (IU) of vitamin D—an important vitamin commonly generated when sunlight strikes the skin—may decrease the risk of common cancers by 50 percent. Although some foods, such as orange juice, are now fortified with vitamin D, it is hard to get enough from a regular diet. For example, a glass of milk contains only 100 IU. The researchers recommend taking a vitamin D supplement along with eating a healthy diet and getting limited sun exposure as the best way to get enough of this important cancer protection.

Not all cancers can be prevented, but experts agree that by adopting a healthy lifestyle, people can significantly reduce their cancer risk. The Department of Health and Human Services says that the number of new cancer cases could be reduced and many cancer deaths could be prevented if everyone followed these effective cancer prevention measures:

Avoiding tobacco
Avoiding sun exposure
Improving nutrition
Increasing physical activity
Achieving optimal weight[12]

Surviving Cancer

It is encouraging to know that some cancers can be prevented. It is even more encouraging to know that millions of people who have been diagnosed with cancer are living full and satisfying lives. Among cancer survivors are many celebrities: athletes, political leaders, prominent businesspeople, musicians, stage and movie actors, and TV personalities. Some of these rich and famous survivors have used their wealth and status to help other victims of cancer. Their stories are inspiring, but so are the stories of the millions of less well-known cancer survivors who have battled cancer and refused to let it control their lives.

The Lance Armstrong Story

In May 2008, when Lance Armstrong was named one of *Time* magazine's "100 Most Influential People," Elizabeth Edwards— mother of four, author, breast cancer survivor, and wife of former presidential candidate John Edwards—wrote this tribute:

> There is no one else quite like him. And there probably never will be. The best cyclist ever, Lance Armstrong won the sport's premier event, the Tour de France, an almost incomprehensible seven times from 1999 to 2005. But before he could do that, in 1996 he had to beat back a cancer that was supposed to take his life. Testicular cancer had spread to his abdomen, lungs and brain. Grim-faced doctors told him he had no chance. But "no chance" were not words that had meaning for Lance.[13]

In 1996 cyclist Lance Armstrong was diagnosed with testicular cancer. After four cycles of chemotherapy, he was pronounced clear of cancer.

When Lance Armstrong was diagnosed with testicular cancer in 1996, his symptoms were some pain in a testicle and coughing up some blood. He underwent an ultrasound examination that revealed a testicular tumor. Then he underwent chest X-rays and a brain scan that revealed the cancer had spread to his lungs, stomach, and brain. After two surgeries to remove the cancerous testicle and the two metastatic cancers in his brain, he underwent four cycles of chemotherapy. He suffered the usual side effects of nausea, hair loss, fatigue, and weakening of his immune system. But once the chemo was finished and he was pronounced clear of cancer, he went back to training for his next bicycle race. Determined to put his experience to good use, he started the Lance Armstrong Foundation to provide resources and support services to people diagnosed with cancer and their families. The foundation's services include Cycle of Hope, a national cancer education campaign for people with cancer and those at risk for developing the disease. The foundation also maintains a Web site where cancer survivors share their experiences, and it provides research grants to help scientists study the disease.

Joyce Kulhawik and the Daffodils

One week before her wedding in 1979, Joyce Kulhawik noticed a suspicious mole on her thigh. A biopsy showed it was a malignant melanoma. She walked down the aisle with her leg in seventeen stitches, which her husband removed on their honeymoon. Nine years later, while practicing yoga, Kulhawik experienced a high temperature, chills, and abdominal pain. Doctors gave her antibiotics and two weeks later decided to operate on her appendix. Instead of appendicitis, they discovered a tumor on her left ovary. The cancerous ovary was removed. A year later Joyce experienced more pain and had emergency surgery to remove her remaining ovary, which was also cancerous.

Kulhawik is a former arts and entertainment reporter at WBZ-TV in Boston and a popular TV personality in Massachusetts. Like Armstrong, she decided to use her high profile and cancer experience to help others. In 1991 Kulhawik testified before Congress about her own cancer experience and the importance of increasing the budget for cancer research. Kulhawik herself has helped raise $10 million for the ACS. Each spring for twenty years, Kulhawik has chaired the American Cancer Society's Daffodil Days—a fund-raising drive to raise

money to support cancer research, education, and service programs. During the drive daffodils are sold as a symbol of hope.
In 2008, 3 million flowers were sold.

Every year Kulhawik visits schools—from day care centers
to universities—hospitals, women's groups, and art gatherings,
talking to thousands of people. At the schools, children dress
in daffodil costumes and write stories about how cancer has
touched their lives. Kulhawik tells them, "Cancer is very much
a part of who I am. Basically we're all in this together. Cancer
has affected every single person on the planet. Either you have
it yourself, or you know someone who does, a family member
or friend. Everybody has a cancer story."[14]

Veronica McBride, a cancer patient, is surrounded by dozens
of daffodils as part of the American Cancer Society fund-raiser
known as Daffodil Days, chaired by Joyce Kulhawik.

Tyler Walton and Harry Potter

At the age of five, Tyler Walton was diagnosed with leukemia. With treatment, the cancer went into remission. But when he was eight he had a relapse, and the leukemia came back worse than before. He had a stroke, a perforated bowel, and fungus in his lungs and his brain. For almost a year, he didn't walk and had to be fed through a tube. Finally, after a bone marrow transplant from his little sister, he began to recover.

When a local newspaper announced an essay contest, Tyler wrote about his experience with cancer. "My life has not been easy," his essay began. He told about being treated for cancer, and how his mother would snuggle with him in his hospital bed and read to him the novels about Harry Potter, the young orphaned wizard created by British author J.K. Rowling. "Harry Potter helped me get through some really hard and scary times," Tyler said of the boy wizard who faces momentous dangers and adult-sized villains. "I sometimes think of Harry Potter and me as being kind of alike. He was forced into situations he couldn't control and had to face an enemy that he didn't know if he could beat." Tyler's essay was one of ten winners chosen out of ten thousand entries, and he got to meet J.K. Rowling, who whispered a secret in his ear about what would happen in the next book. Tyler's essay concluded, "I know I will do fine and so will Harry Potter because good always wins against evil."

Quoted in "Harry Potter and Tyler Walton, the Boys Who Lived," ACS News Center, December 26, 2001, www.cancer.org/docroot/FPS/content/FPS_1_Harry_Potter_and_Tyler_Walton_the_Boys_Who_Lived.asp?SiteArea=.

Louise S.

Some cancer survivors try to put the experience behind them and would rather not talk about it. Others, like Louise S., are willing to share their feelings about what has been helpful and what has not. Louise was diagnosed with rhabdomyosarcoma (RMS) at the age of nine. In 1970 little research had been done on the disease, which affects the soft tissue and can be deadly. It can grow anywhere in the body, but is most often found in the head or neck, the abdomen, or an arm or leg. She and eight other children nationwide were pioneers on whom new treatment was tried.

When Louise had surgery in Dallas to remove as much of the tumor as possible, it was discovered that the tumor in her head went into the bone surrounding her right eye. Her eye was not removed, but she lost sight in it. At the M.D. Anderson Cancer Center in Houston, Texas, Louise was treated with radiation and combination chemotherapy. The chemo was an extremely experimental treatment at the time, as doctors were trying to find a combination that was effective for treating RMS. Three of her teeth were fused to her jawbone by radiation. In the spring of 2008, when she was forty-eight, one of the teeth became infected and had to be pulled. For a short time she was terrified that if anything went wrong she might lose part of her jaw. Fortunately, that didn't happen.

Louise feels that in order to survive cancer it is important for children to know the truth about their disease. She says:

> Sugar coating the truth is the last thing that we need. The majority of the time, whatever the future may hold, we will probably end up having to wear it on our bodies; whether it's amputation, problems with our teeth, infertility, premature menopause, or in some cases, breasts not forming on a young adult woman. These are not things that will go away if our parents don't tell us about them, and we need plenty of time to decide how we will cope with these things when they come. My mother was very straightforward with me and that helped me to understand what I had to do to survive.

> Recently, on a survey they asked the question, "How did you find your 'new normal'?" I found that offensive because, once again it prevents us from dealing with some of the hard facts about surviving. We look different, we

sound different, and we've seen an aspect of life and death that few children see. My idea of normal was the person that I had been before cancer. I knew that she was gone and I was going to have to figure out who was left.[15]

Laura A.

Laura A. considers having cancer a "gift" that changed her life for the better. In October 2004 Laura was diagnosed with high-grade chondroblastic osteosarcoma (bone cancer) of the right maxilla (cheekbone) with no metastasis. This is a rare cancer that typically occurs in adolescents, but she was thirty-eight. She received four cycles of chemotherapy followed by surgery. The treatments lasted about six months.

Cancer patients cannot control their disease, but they can control their response to the disease. A positive outlook helps many patients deal with the struggles of treatment.

During the course of her treatments, she encountered physical changes, including hair loss, weight loss, and surgery scars. Since treatment, she has had to adjust to permanent changes in her body, including hearing loss and organ damage, among others. She has also had to learn new ways to chew food. The experience was physically difficult and at times very scary.

Laura says:

As I started my journey into "cancer world," I was in mental shock, and even angry, but as my treatment began, that mental shock and anger changed into something unexpected. This may sound strange, but I have come to believe that my cancer was a gift. Some of the aspects of my "gift" were and are bad. In fact, I could go on and on about all the lousy things that happened to me during and after cancer treatment. But some of the aspects of my gift, or "opportunity," were and are wonderful.

Before cancer, an outsider would have looked at my life and determined that I had a very good one—a loving husband, supportive family and friends, solid career path, good health, a nice home, a plethora of material possessions, nice vacations, etc. However, since my childhood (beginning at about the age of eleven) there began a deep feeling of insecurity and melancholy simmering in the background. I became highly critical of myself and deeply unhappy with myself, despite all the many blessings that surrounded me. Sometimes I would get so focused on the negative that I would become very depressed. Unfortunately, these negative feelings and outlook continued with me throughout my adolescence and on into my adulthood.

Cancer completely changed that. Not long after being diagnosed, I realized that I had the power to choose my attitude—to give up or fight, to be positive or negative. And although I didn't know which to choose at first—in fact, I initially thought that I was cursed and it was my destiny to die young—I fairly quickly decided that I did want to fight for my life and that I was going to focus on the positive.

Some days, I'll admit, it was very difficult to do so. Having a loving and supportive family greatly helped me with this, but I was the one with the power over my mental choice and no one else. I realized that I was the one making me miserable all along for all of those years, and that I had tremendous power over my attitude and approach to life. I found that my newfound positive outlook, despite the dire circumstances, was very helpful to me, and even inspirational to those around me.

I wouldn't describe my newfound attitude as seeing the world through rose-colored glasses. I realize that horrible things happen that are beyond our control, and that I was very fortunate to find my cancer early, get a proper diagnosis, and find experienced doctors with a clear treatment plan. Not all cancer stories end as well as mine—and even this realization has made my experience that much more precious and meaningful to me.

All in all, I am so very grateful for my unwanted "gift." I may have two more years to live; I may live to ninety, like both my grandmothers. Either way, I remind myself each day of my life that my attitude is my choice. I am going to *choose* to be grateful. I am going to *choose* to be kind and compassionate to others. Not because I think I should be, but because it makes me happy, and I hope it will be infectious.[16]

C.J. Howard

C.J. Howard was an athlete, running sixty-five to seventy miles a week, when he developed a bad pain in his heel. An MRI showed a small growth on the heel, and he also had a stress fracture. Doctors told him to take six weeks off from running. The next year he started running for the University of California, Irvine, and midway through the season his heel started hurting again. Another MRI showed that the growth had increased from about half a centimeter to four or five centimeters. His doctor referred him to a specialist, who scheduled him for a biopsy.

Olympic Swimmer Lives with Cancer

In late spring of 2008, just a week before the Olympic trials, U.S. swimmer Eric Shanteau learned that he had testicular cancer. "I was sort of like, 'This isn't real. There's no way this is happening to me right now,'" Shanteau said. "You're trying to get ready for the Olympics, and you just get this huge bomb dropped on you." When doctors determined his cancer had not spread, the twenty-four-year-old athlete went to the trials and made the team. He decided to put off surgery until after he had been to Beijing and fulfilled his dream of swimming in the Olympics.

Quoted in Paul Newberry, "Cancer Can't Stop Swimmer's Olympic Dream," *Temple Daily Telegram*, July 12, 2008.

On December 23, 2002, he was diagnosed with osteosarcoma, a common type of bone cancer. He went through months of chemotherapy. The treatments made him very nauseated, a feeling he hated. Then the oncologist said he needed an amputation. Howard says,

The amputation was something that, originally, I had tricked myself into thinking that I was okay with. But I wasn't always so positive during the next three-and-a-half months. I think I was lucky to have those months, and that it wasn't so immediate. I got to say, "I'm okay with it." And I got to say, "No, I'm not okay with it." I got to cry about it. I basically went through the acceptance process before it happened, which I think helped a lot. Because as soon as it did happen, I think my mindset changed a lot. So on April 28th, four months later, I had the surgery and was up walking the next day with crutches and everything.[17]

Howard's leg was amputated below the knee. He accepted the amputation as another physical challenge, just like running. After three weeks in a cast and then another three weeks waiting for the swelling in the leg (caused by the surgery) to shrink down, he got an artificial foot. It took him only three days to start walking without crutches. Then a local nonprofit organization called Fulfill-A-Dream granted his wish for a running prosthesis. He started running on the prosthesis before he had even regrown the hair he lost during chemotherapy.

In the spring of 2004, he set the national record in the 5K, and he set personal records in the 5000 meters. He ran his first 5K in twenty-five minutes, and within six months ran it in eighteen and a half minutes. Howard feels an obligation to be a positive influence on other people. He says, "I've had something that many people would describe as terrible, but it's also given me the opportunity to make an impact in other people's lives. Every time that I'm running and somebody sees me, they're like, 'You're a major influence,' or 'You inspire me,' that's what I want to do."[18]

Doctors Get Cancer, Too

Mark Liponis was a hard-driving young doctor, focused on building a secure future for his family. It had never occurred to him that he might get one of the diseases he was treating. His parents, the children of Greek immigrants, had taught him that the path to success was created by hard work and a strong will. At thirty-six he was not prepared for the detour life threw at him—cancer.

The only ominous symptom he had was a single episode of painless, bloody urine during a late shift in the ER one night. Tests showed an apple-sized tumor in his left kidney. He was quickly scheduled for surgery to remove his kidney and surrounding lymph nodes. He was shocked to learn that the tumor had been growing for about fifteen years. Today, thirteen years after his diagnosis, he has a successful medical career. His experience has led him to want to share what he learned with others:

Standard medical treatment is just one part of overcoming cancer. Surviving is a four-part process that includes treatment, healing, prevention, and life extension. But the steps many of us associate with cancer prevention (a healthy diet, exercise, proper sleep, stress management, smoking cessation, and moderation of habits) are also critical during the stages of treatment, healing, and the years that follow. I learned that these are the most effective ways of keeping microscopic cancer cells from growing into serious tumors.[19]

The Last Lecture Professor

A professor of computer science at Carnegie Mellon University, Randy Pausch was a pioneer of virtual reality research. In September 2006, when he was forty-five, he was diagnosed with pancreatic cancer. A year later, he gave a speech titled "Really Achieving Your Childhood Dreams" to a standing-room-only crowd. It was part of a series Carnegie Mellon had orginally called *The Last Lecture*, in which professors were asked to give a hypothetical final talk about what mattered to them most.

The speech became an Internet sensation and was expanded into a best-selling book that Pausch dictated by cell phone to *Wall Street Journal* writer Jeffrey Zaslow. In the lecture and in the book, Pausch discussed the experience of facing terminal cancer—and he talked about achieving dreams. He said, "How well we live matters more than how long we live. . . . Obstacles give us a chance to show how badly we want something. . . . It's not about how to achieve your dreams, it's about how to lead your life. . . . If you lead your life the right way, the karma will take care of itself, the dreams will come to you."[20] Ten months after giving the lecture, Randy Pausch died at his home in Chesapeake, Virginia. His book remained at the top of the nonfiction best-seller lists.

Resources for Cancer Survivors

A diagnosis of cancer is a traumatic experience for anyone, but today there are many helpful resources, services, and support

Randy Pausch gives his final lecture on time management before a packed house on November 27, 2007, in Charlottesville, Virginia.

groups available. Patients are fortunate if they have a strong, supportive circle of family and friends. Clergy and counselors and teachers can also be of help. Internet friends who have undergone similar experiences can be very valuable in helping deal with the physical and emotional challenges of the disease. In addition, there are many national and local support groups for cancer survivors.

National Cancer Survivors Day (NCSD) is an annual worldwide celebration held in hundreds of communities each year to demonstrate that life after a cancer diagnosis is a reality. The nonprofit National Cancer Survivors Day Foundation supports hospitals, support groups, and other cancer-related organizations that host NCSD events. Traditionally, NCSD is observed on the first Sunday in June. The theme is up to the sponsoring host. For example, on June 1, 2008, in Temple, Texas, the Scott & White Hospital, the Temple Veterans Administration Hospital, the American Cancer Society, and the

Yul Brynner Lives On

A quarter of a century ago Yul Brynner was one of the most famous actors in the world. He made a number of movies that became classics. He also smoked continually, and he developed lung cancer. In 1985, knowing he was dying, he made a commercial for TV. It showed a burning cigarette with a ban mark through it, and Brynner's picture. The message was: "NOW THAT I'M GONE, I TELL YOU: DON'T SMOKE, WHATEVER YOU DO, JUST DON'T SMOKE." Before his death, he also arranged for the establishment of the Yul Brynner Head and Neck Cancer Foundation, which has chapters in many states.

Susan G. Komen Foundation held a "Hawaiian Luau" for cancer survivors. Attendees wore their favorite festive tropical outfits. Activities included costume and hula hoop contests, along with other games, a Hawaiian buffet, and gifts.

In addition to Daffodil Days, the American Cancer Society sponsors other activities intended to celebrate survivorship and raise money for cancer research.

Relay for Life is a fun-filled overnight event during which teams take turns walking or running laps at schools, fairgrounds, or parks. Long-term survivors, newly diagnosed patients, caregivers, and friends participate. National and regional corporations also organize teams. In 2008 Relay for Life events were held in eighteen countries around the world.

Coaches vs. Cancer is a nationwide joint collaboration between the American Cancer Society and the National Association of Basketball Coaches (NABC). It started with one cancer survivor, Norm Stewart, former head coach of the University of Missouri's men's basketball program. He began the program by challenging fans to pledge a dollar amount for every three-point shot made by his team during the season. In 1993 the ACS and the NABC adopted the idea and made it into a nationwide effort to unite coaches across the country in a mission to provide help and hope to people fighting cancer.

Other Resources

The Internet offers a number of opportunities for cancer survivors to find information and connect with other survivors. As with any good thing, there are dishonest people willing to put out false information for personal gain, so it is wise to check the sponsor or source of information on the Web carefully. The American Cancer Society has a Web-based service for cancer survivors at www.acscan.org. The network provides survivors and families access to live online chat sessions, virtual support groups, prerecorded talk shows, and personal stories. Another helpful resource is the fact sheet that can be obtained by contacting the National Cancer Institute. It lists many cancer organizations that can provide information about support groups. The Lance Armstrong Foundation is also a good resource for information for cancer survivors.

The American Cancer Society's Relay for Life is a major fund-raising event drawing thousands of participants each year.

There are a number of camps throughout the United States that provide activities that give children who are fighting cancer relief from the frustrations of being treated for cancer and an opportunity to feel like a normal kid again. The Hole in the Wall Gang Camp, founded by actor Paul Newman, offers nine summer sessions free of charge. This superbly equipped Wild West hideout in Connecticut hosts more than one thousand children from ages seven to fifteen each year.

Camp Ronald McDonald for Good Times conducts summer and winter camps for young cancer patients as well as spring and fall family camps for families who have a child with cancer. Sibling camps provide the same fun and support for the brothers and sisters of cancer patients. Swimming, horseback riding, hiking, backpacking, and other activities are adapted so that each child is able to participate.

Brian's Song

Sometimes when a cancer patient loses his struggle with the disease, the memory of his fight survives and lives on to inspire others. This was true of Brian Piccolo, whose story was made into a TV movie in 1971. In high school, Piccolo became a football star. Then he signed a free-agent contract with the Chicago Bears. He dreamed of becoming a great NFL running back. But just when he seemed to be within reach of this goal, he had a series of injuries, including a ruptured cartilage and a pulled hamstring. The other obstacle was his good friend and roommate, Gale Sayers. Sayers was such a superstar as a running back, Piccolo had to settle for being Sayers's backup most of the time.

When chest pains and a persistent cough grounded him, Piccolo had a chest X-ray that revealed a tumor in his lung. When he underwent surgery to remove the malignant tumor, doctors found that it had spread. He began chemotherapy, and in the spring of 1970 his left lung and left breast were removed. He told reporters he would return to play football again. When Sayers won the NFL rushing title and was honored at a ceremony in New York, he told the audience that Piccolo was the

Brian Piccolo's battle with cancer was made into an inspirational movie called *Brian's Song*.

one who should be receiving an award. His best friend, he told them, had the heart of a lion and a rare form of courage. A few weeks later, Piccolo was readmitted to the hospital with chest pains, and he died soon after.

The movie *Brian's Song*, which tells Piccolo's story, became a classic overnight. Since 1971 it has been remade and expanded, and generations later people still shed tears at this moving story of friendship and courage. Since his death, the Brian Piccolo Cancer Research Fund has raised more than $5 million.

Many celebrities whose family lives have been affected by cancer use their fame to raise awareness of cancer. For example, supermodel Cindy Crawford makes appearances to raise awareness of pediatric cancer. Her younger brother, Jeff, died of leukemia in 1975, before his fourth birthday. Crawford is the honorary chair of Kids with Courage, which held its fourth reunion of childhood cancer survivors June 5, 2008. Jeff was a patient at University of Wisconsin Children's Hospital, and for nearly twenty years his sister has contributed time and money to the university's pediatric oncology program.

Across the nation and around the world, there are numerous foundations and individuals working to raise funds for cancer research in the names of cancer victims. And numerous scholarships have been established in the names of cancer victims. These scholarships provide opportunities for young men and women who will go on to be teachers and researchers, and perhaps discover ways to finally defeat this devastating disease.

CHAPTER FIVE

The Future Outlook for Cancer

Since President Richard Nixon signed the National Cancer Act in 1971, billions of dollars have been spent in the United States to fight the War on Cancer. Better ways of diagnosing and preventing cancer and of treating and caring for cancer patients have been discovered. Millions of cancer patients have survived much longer than would have been possible even a few decades ago. The war, however, is far from over, although tremendous progress has been made and a number of battles have been won. In this never-ending fight, older therapies are being refined and practically reinvented. In addition, outstanding scientists all over the world are exploring a number of exciting possibilities for improved diagnosis, treatment, and prevention of this dreaded disease.

Targeted Therapies

For many years, surgery, chemotherapy, and radiation have been the standard methods used to treat cancer. Radiation works by causing DNA changes in cells. High doses effectively kill cancer cells, but even relatively low doses can cause changes in normal cells and may cause them to become cancerous. Before the dangers of radiation were fully understood, many early radiologists developed leukemia. Through research, radiation therapy is constantly improving. Now, concentrated beams of radiation are focused directly on the tumor site. This technique reduces the risk of harming adjacent tissues and also increases the dose that can safely be given.

Chemotherapy has also been a double-edged sword. It is usually given as a mix of toxic drugs that circulate through the body and kill rapidly dividing cells. Unfortunately, the drugs also interact with normal cells and can have moderate to severe side effects. In the past, doctors had no choice but to try to choose a dose that would kill the cancer cells before the

Protesters demonstrate against the closing of medical marijuana clinics in Los Angeles County, California, in 2008. The use of medical marijuana to help with side effects caused by cancer treatments is controversial.

toxic drugs killed the patient. New drugs are more effective in destroying cancer while doing less harm to healthy cells.

The advanced chemotherapy used today can still have disagreeable side effects. However, research is discovering ways to help patients tolerate them better, and modern medications make the problem of nausea and vomiting less severe. Antinausea, or antiemetic, drugs are given along with intravenous chemotherapy drugs, and the patient is instructed to take a second dose within an hour after the treatment ends.

Studies have shown that electro-acupuncture, in which pressure points are stimulated by a tiny electric current, may have real value in reducing the nausea that accompanies chemotherapy. Acupressure, where the patient applies pressure to acupuncture points, has also been found valuable in reducing nausea after chemotherapy.

The use of marijuana to relieve nausea, vomiting, and certain kinds of pain associated with cancer and chemotherapy is more controversial. Although some states have passed legislation allowing marijuana use for medical purposes, the Food and Drug Administration continues to insist there is no sound scientific basis for believing marijuana use has medical benefits. There are also studies that link a risk of head and neck cancer to habitual marijuana smoking. American Cancer Society expert Michael Thun agrees with this finding. He says, "Many of the same cancer causing substances in tobacco smoke are present in marijuana smoke. Marijuana cigarettes generally deposit more tar in the respiratory tract than tobacco cigarettes."[21] In 1985 the FDA approved dronabinol, a synthetic form of the active marijuana constituent delta-9-tetrahydrocannabinol (marketed as Marinol), as a prescription drug for use as an antiemetic. The pros and cons of the use of marijuana by cancer patients continue to be debated in Congress, in the news media, and on the Internet.

Targeted Drugs

Many people, including scientists, consider targeted drugs to be the wave of the future. Gleevec was the first of these drugs approved by the Food and Drug Administration. It represents a new class of drugs and introduced a new way of thinking about cancer. Beginning in 1998, clinical trials showed dramatic responses to Gleevec in patients with advanced stages of cancer. In 2001 Gleevec was approved by the FDA for treatment of chronic myeloid leukemia, a cancer of white blood cells, and it was approved for the treatment of a form of stomach cancer called gastrointestinal stromal tumor (GIST) in 2002. Gleevec and other targeted drugs are designed to zero in on specific cancer-causing proteins. They destroy cancer cells but do not do serious damage to normal cells.

Tamoxifen is another targeted drug that has received a great deal of publicity. When it was first introduced, it was hailed by some doctors and patients as a miracle drug. Most breast cancers grow in response to estrogen. Tamoxifen works by blocking estrogen receptors on breast cancer cells. Studies showed that giving patients tamoxifen after breast cancer surgery reduced the chance that the cancer would return. Women were advised by their doctors to take tamoxifen for five years.

When it was found that the benefits of tamoxifen faded over time, allowing the cancer to start growing again, scientists at Duke University Medical Center proposed an explanation. The researchers suggested that tamoxifen initially works by preventing estrogen from binding to receptors in breast cells. The drug changes the shape of the receptors and prevents them from taking part in the process of cancer cell growth. Eventually, the report said, the cells adapt and recognize tamoxifen as an "estrogen," allowing cell growth to proceed. Since the resistance to tamoxifen usually develops in two to five years, there seems to be little benefit in taking the drug for more than five years.

Almost immediately, another targeted drug came to the rescue. An article in the *New England Journal of Medicine* reported that "women who switched to the drug exemestane after 2 or 3 years of tamoxifen were less likely to see their cancer return than women who stayed on tamoxifen the full 5 years."[22] Other experts argue that it is too early to know whether exemestane and drugs like it are a better choice for some breast cancer survivors.

Obviously, the field of targeted drugs is still in its infancy, but the drugs' potential in fighting cancer is exciting. A step beyond simply developing and using targeted drugs is making them into designer drugs. Researchers now have the ability to profile cancer genes, examine them to see what makes them abnormal, and search for ways to disrupt their abnormal behavior. Doctors are able to personalize treatment by using specific drugs for people with a particular combination of defective genes. For example, Herceptin is used to treat certain types of breast cancer. About one-third of breast cancer patients have a gene called HER2, which causes cells to produce extra receptors, resulting in uncontrolled growth. Herceptin blocks these receptors, targeting only cells covered with huge numbers of the receptors. A test for the HER2 gene has been

Gleevec was the first targeted drug to be approved by the United States Food and Drug Administration. Patients suffering from chronic myeloid leukemia and a stomach cancer called gastrointestinal stroma tumor (GIST) have responded well to the drug.

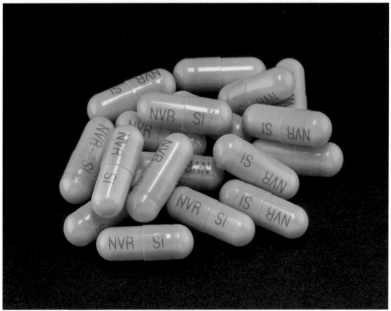

developed, which means doctors can prescribe Herceptin for exactly the breast cancer patients who can benefit from it.

Immunotherapy

Today, much cancer research is focused on the human immune system. Researchers are working to discover how the immune system functions to prevent cancer and how it can be used to cure cancer. Normally the immune system acts as the body's defense system, fighting cancer cells and keeping the body cancer-free by attacking the cells before they can grow and spread. When the immune system is weakened, it cannot do its job effectively. Immunotherapy (also known as biotherapy) takes advantage of the body's own ability to fight disease. It is aimed at strengthening the patient's immune system and helping it recognize cancer cells as undesirable aliens. Immunotherapy uses a number of different techniques.

Interferons are substances normally used by the body to fight viruses. They can be used to fight cancer by inhibiting the division of cancer cells so that they become sluggish and die. Artificially introduced interferons are powerful medicine. They stimulate antibody-producing B cells, killer T cells, and macrophages, which are white blood cells that gobble up foreign cells. As with many potent treatments, interferon treatments can have a number of unpleasant side effects. These may include temporary flulike symptoms and long-term problems such as chronic fatigue, memory loss, and depression.

Vaccines are another form of immunotherapy under intense investigation. Chemicals called antigens are usually found on the surface of cancer cells. Dead tumor cells that still have their surface antigens are used to make vaccines, but the antigens alone also may be used. The antigen vaccine is then injected into the body in an effort to prompt an immune response against the cancer.

Melanoma is one type of cancer that responds well to therapy that boosts immune responses against cancer. In Australia, which has the world's highest skin cancer rate, clinical trials with vaccines are being conducted, and the results are encouraging. Tim Stobo of Ballarat, Australia, enjoys golfing, surfing, and sailing. His regular exposure to the sun caused him to develop melanoma. After undergoing surgery and radiation, he joined the vaccine trials. When asked by a reporter how the trials were going, he said, "The people are very good. I ask semi-intelligent questions, they give responses I can understand, suggest reading I can do. They treat me like a researcher, in a way. And I have high hopes for the vaccine."[23]

Pictured here is vial of interferon, which is used to inhibit the growth of cancer cells.

Antiangiogenesis

Much cancer research is being centered on antiangiogenesis. Angiogenesis, the formation of new blood vessels in the body, is a normal process. Blood vessels are needed to supply cells with the oxygen and nutrients they must have to live and grow. As a tumor gets bigger, its center cells get farther and farther from the blood vessels in the area where it is growing. Scientists now think a cancer tumor cannot grow much bigger than a pencil tip before it has to develop its own blood supply. Cancer cells send out signals to activate genes to produce proteins that stimulate the growth of capillaries. Once a tumor can stimulate the growth of new blood vessels, it can grow very quickly and stimulate the growth of hundreds of new capillaries to bring it nutrients and oxygen.

Experts now believe angiogenesis may also explain why a secondary cancer can appear years after the primary cancer has been discovered and treated. The tiny secondary tumor may have lain dormant without a supply of oxygen or nutrients. Then, through mutation, the cells may suddenly be able to trigger capillary growth, and the cancer comes to life and begins growing rapidly.

By inhibiting tumor angiogenesis, a basic requirement for malignant growth is blocked. The challenge is to find drugs that will interfere with the ability of a cancerous tumor to stimulate blood vessel growth. A number of inhibitor drugs are available, and scientists are working to find the most effective ways to use them to starve cancer cells without causing undesirable side effects for the patient. Examples of drugs under study for the purpose of antiangiogenesis are interferon alpha, avastin, and thalidomide.

In the early 1960s, thalidomide acquired a bad reputation. For years European doctors had prescribed it as a mild sleep aid and antinausea remedy. After thousands of women who had taken the drug to ease their morning sickness gave birth to babies with tiny flippers instead of arms and legs, it was withdrawn from the market. Recently it has made a comeback as an angiogenesis inhibitor. Researchers have found that the

Cancer Research

There are numerous cancer research organizations, large and small, in many countries worldwide. Some are connected with hospitals and other treatment centers and some operate independently. The National Institutes of Health is an important United States agency devoted to medical research. It operates under the Department of Health and Human Services and consists of twenty-seven separate institutes and centers. Among them is the National Cancer Institute. The mission of the NCI is

> to lead a national effort to reduce the burden of cancer morbidity and mortality and ultimately to prevent the disease. Through basic and clinical biomedical research and training, NCI conducts and supports programs to understand the causes of cancer; prevent, detect, diagnose, treat, and control cancer; and disseminate information to the practitioner, patient, and public.

> The NCI's Cancer Information Service is a national information and education network for patients, the public, and health professionals. From regional offices covering the entire United States, trained staff provide the latest cancer information through a toll-free telephone service.

Quoted in "Definition of National Cancer Institute (NCI)" www.medterms.com/script/main/art.asp?articlekey=6780.

drug, which stunted limb develoment in embryos by blocking the formation of blood vessels, could also stunt the growth of tumors. In 2006 thalidomide received FDA approval, and the villain returned as a hero.

Genetic Research

Scientists are just beginning to tap into genetics and the profiling of cancer genes. Since it is a change in a person's DNA that causes cancer, some think that a cure for cancer may lie in the human genetic code. Gabriel N. Hortobagyi, director of the multidisciplinary breast cancer research program at the University of Texas M.D. Anderson Cancer Center in Houston, says, "For the past 50 years oncologists tested hundreds of thousands of compounds on cancer cells to see if they would slow the growth or destroy them. It was very inefficient. Now

Scientists are using genetics to identify those who have an increased risk of developing cancer.

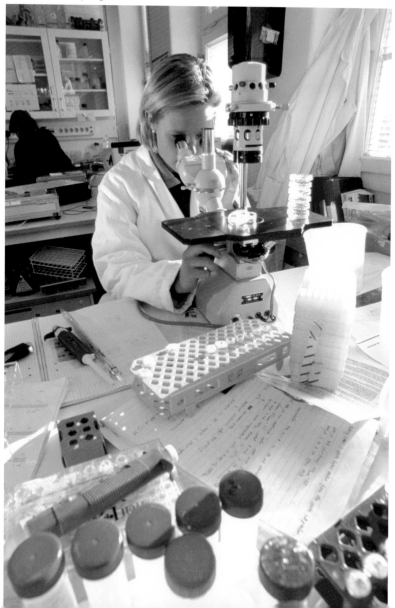

we can profile cancer genes, understand what makes them abnormal, then look for very specific ways to disrupt those processes. This is a revolution. Instead of developing 50 drugs over 50 years, we're developing 10 or 20 drugs every year."[24]

In April 2008 researchers announced that they had identified genetic quirks that increase the risk of lung cancer in smokers and former smokers. Three international teams each pinpointed the same genetic link to cancer risk. Their findings on genetic links are a major breakthrough that will help researchers identify people who are at high risk for non-small cell lung cancer, the most common form of the disease. Identifying those at high risk is important, because there are usually no symptoms until the cancer is in an advanced stage.

Carcinogen Research

In the future, doctors may be able to replace defective genes before a person develops cancer. In the meantime, the search goes on for substances that can cause changes in cells that may lead to cancer. The cancer research branch of the World Health Organization tests and evaluates agents that have cancer-causing potential. Out of about nine hundred substances they have tested, about ninety are classified as "carcinogenic to humans."[25] The National Toxicology Program in the United States releases a report on carcinogens every two years. The report divides the tested agents into those known to be human carcinogens and those that are probably carcinogenic to humans.

Debates arise almost every day concerning the possible danger of suspected cancer-causing agents. Recent stories about nanotubes claim that they are as dangerous as asbestos. The federal government has heavily funded the development of nanotechnology, which involves the use of particles a few billionths of a meter in diameter. Carbon nanotubes have become the basic building blocks utilized in the making of some electronic components, appliances, toys, and dozens of other products. Preliminary evidence of their cancer-causing potential in tests with mice is strong enough to cause concern for workers in nanotech factories. In an article in the journal

A man holds a bottle of nanotubes. Nanotubes are important in the building of many products, including appliances and toys, but may also be a carcinogen.

Nature Nanotechnology, researcher Anthony Seaton said, "In a sense we are forewarned and forearmed now with respect to nanotubes. We know that some of them probably have the potential to cause mesothelioma [a fatal form of cancer]. So those sorts of materials need to be handled very carefully."[26]

Alternative Treatments

When traditional ways of treating cancer through surgery, chemotherapy, and radiation do not seem to be working or become difficult to take, some patients turn to alternative treatments. These may include radical diets, herbal remedies, yoga, acupuncture, and homeopathy. (Homeopathy is a method of treating a disease by giving patients a minute amount of a substance that causes symptoms similar to those resulting from the disease.)

In May 2008, medical journalist Susan Aldridge reported, "A survey within Europe reveals that one cancer patient in three is using some kind of complementary or alternative medicine. The number in the United States is even higher, and users tend to be younger, [to be] female and to have cancer of the bone, brain, pancreas or liver—in other words, those cancers with a poorer prognosis."[27]

A homeopath prepares remedies. Homeopathy is an alternative treatment for diseases like cancer.

The National Cancer Institute reviews and tests alternative treatments to determine whether they are effective. One concern is that the alternative treatments may have harmful side effects that outweigh any possible benefit. Other alternative treatments may be safe but have little or no benefit. According to cancer doctors, the gravest danger is that patients using alternative treatments may give up standard treatments that might be more effective in fighting the disease. The medical community currently does not accept many alternative approaches, despite the fact that there are cancer survivors who believe that alternative treatments have saved their lives. The research and the debates over alternative treatments continue. One possible result is that some alternative treatments may be combined with traditional treatments to make life easier for the patient.

A Cure for Cancer?

Soon after the United States government declared the War on Cancer, there was much talk of discovering a "magic bullet" that would seek out and destroy cancer cells throughout the body. That dream has still not become reality. There are so many differences among the several hundred diseases that are called cancer, it seems unlikely that any one treatment will be useful in all cases. However, scientists have acquired a tremendous amount of knowledge about how each cancer occurs and about the possibilities of curing it. As Paraic A. Kenny says in *Stages of Cancer Development*, "Although we may never find that so-called magic bullet, we will soon have an array of mini-bullets that we can mix-and-match depending on the characteristics of the individual tumor. It is hoped that these cocktails will prove much more effective than the 'cut it out, burn it out, and poison it' approach of surgery, radiation therapy, and chemotherapy."[28]

While researchers work around the clock to develop successful mini-bullets to seek and destroy cancers, there are a number of ways people can help protect themselves. People can avoid known risk factors as much as possible. They can

Stem Cells

Stem cells may be a key to unlocking some of the mysteries still lying behind the complicated disease known as cancer. There are two basic types of stem cells. Embryonic stem cells usually come from fertilized eggs that have been discarded after a fertility treatment. When an egg is fertilized, it begins to divide. After about five days, the egg is a collection of about 150 cells known as a blastocyst. The inner cells of the blastocyst are stem cells that can grow into any type of cell in the body. Research on the uses of human embryonic stem cells has been restricted by legislation.

Scientists have used adult stem cells for therapeutic purposes for more than three decades. They are found in many places in the body, but they are not as versatile as embryonic stem cells. The adult stem cells can only form a closely related family of cells. One advantage of adult stem cells is that they can come from within an individual's own body, making it less likely they will be rejected by the patient's immune system.

One example of how these stem cells are being used is in bone marrow mini-transplants. The donated cells multiply and gradually take over the bone marrow. So far stem cell transplants, or grafts, have worked best in treating patients with chronic myeloid leukemia.

stay healthy by exercising and maintaining a healthy weight. They can reduce fat intake to less than 25 percent of total daily calories and eat vegetables, fruit, and whole grains every day.

People can also stay informed about the progress being made against this disease. Everyone can learn about the local organizations in their areas that offer support and resources to cancer victims. And perhaps some can find a way to join the fight to end the long struggle against this killer.

Notes

Introduction: Cells Gone Wild

1. Quoted in "It Wasn't All Bad," *Week*, May 30, 2008, p. 4.
2. Donna M. Bozzone, foreword to *Stages of Cancer Development*. New York: Chelsea House, 2007, p. 9.

Chapter One: What Is Cancer?

3. Barbara Basler, "Good News About Cancer," *AARP Bulletin*, May 2008, p. 12.

Chapter Two: Detecting and Treating Cancer

4. Wilma R. Caldwell, ed., *Cancer Information for Teens*. Detroit: Omnigraphics, 2004, p. 177.
5. World Health Organization, "Screening for Various Cancers," www.who.int/cancer/detection/variouscancer/en.

Chapter Three: Preventing Cancer

6. Quoted in Caldwell, *Cancer Information for Teens*, p. 77.
7. Quoted in American Cancer Society, "Secondhand Smoke," www.cancer.org/docroot/PED/content/PED_10_2X_Secondhand_Smoke-Clean_Indoor_Air.asp.
8. Quoted in Dennis Thompson, "Radon: The Silent Home Invader That Can Kill," *HealthDay News*, April 4, 2008.
9. Quoted in Takayuki Ishii, *One Thousand Paper Cranes*. New York: Dell Laurel-Leaf, 1997, p. 74.
10. American Cancer Society, "Common Questions About Diet and Cancer," www.cancer.org/docroot/PED/content/PED_3_2X_Common_Questions_About_Diet_and_Cancer.asp?sitearea=PED.
11. American Cancer Society, "Diet and Physical Activity: What's the Cancer Connection?" www.cancer.org/docroot/PED/content/PED_3_1x_Link_Between_Lifestyle_and_CancerMarch03.asp.

12. Department of Health and Human Services, "Preventing
    and Controlling Cancer: The Nation's Second Leading
    Cause of Death," www.cdc.gov/nccdphp/publications/aag/
    dcpc.htm.

Chapter Four: Surviving Cancer

13. Quoted in Lance Armstrong Foundation, "Lance Arm-
    strong Honored as One of *Time's* 100 Most Influential
    People," www.livestrong.org/site/apps/nlnet/content2.aspx
    ?c=khLXK1PxHmF&B=2661079&ct=5320813.
14. Quoted in American Cancer Society, "Like the Daffodils,
    TV Arts Reporter Is a Symbol of Hope," ACS News Center,
    March 27, 2002, www.cancer.org/docroot/FPS/content/
    FPS_1_Like_the_Daffodils_TV_Arts_Reporter_Is_a_
    Symbol_of_Hope.asp?SiteArea=.
15. Louise S., e-mail interviews with author, June 14 and 17,
    2008.
16. Laura A., interviews with author, February 16, May 13,
    and June 12, 2008.
17. Lance Armstrong Foundation, "C.J. Howard Is an Os-
    teosarcoma Survivor," www.livestrong.org/site/apps/
    nlnet/content2.aspx?c=khLXK1PxHmF&b=2661271
    &ct=3755445.
18. Lance Armstrong Foundation, "C.J. Howard Is an Osteo-
    sarcoma Survivor."
19. Mark Liponis, "You Can Survive Cancer (I Did)," *Parade*,
    June 15, 2008, pp. 8–9.
20. Quoted in "Last Lecture Professor Dies at 47," *Temple
    Daily Telegram*, June 26, 2008.

Chapter Five: The Future Outlook for Cancer

21. Quoted in American Cancer Society, "Smoking Marijuana
    May Increase Cancer Risk," ACS News Center, January 18,
    2000, www.cancer.org/docroot/NWS/content/NWS_1_1x_
    Smoking_Marijuana_May_Increase_Cancer_Risk.asp.
22. Quoted in American Cancer Society, "Switch to Exemestane
    Better than Long-Term Tamoxifen in Breast Cancer Study,"
    ACS News Center, March 10, 2004, www.cancer.org/docroot/
    NWS/content/NWS_1_1x_Switch_to_Exemestane_Better_
    than_Long-term_Tamoxifen_in_Breast_Cancer_Study.asp.

23. Quoted in Cancer Research Institute, "Real Stories: Tim Stobo," www.cancerresearch.org/AboutUs.aspx?id=828.

24. Quoted in Basler, "Good News About Cancer," p. 12.

25. Quoted in American Cancer Society, "Known and Probable Carcinogens," www.cancer.org/docroot/PED/content/PED_1_3x_Known_and_Probable_Carcinogens.asp.

26. Quoted in Rick Weiss, "Study: Nanotubes Pose Same Danger as Asbestos," *Washington Post*, May 1, 2008.

27. Susan Aldridge, "One Third of Cancer Patients Using Complementary Therapies," *Health and Age*, May 6, 2008.

28. Paraic A. Kenny, *Stages of Cancer Development.* New York: Chelsea House, 2007, p. 119.

Glossary

angiogenesis: The formation of new blood vessels.

antigens: Proteins on the surface of cells.

benign: The designation of a tumor that is not cancerous.

biopsy: A test in which a tissue sample is removed from a suspicious mass to check for cancer.

carcinogens: Cancer-causing chemicals, such as those found in cigarettes, foods, and industrial materials.

carcinoma: A cancer that starts in the covering and lining tissues in the body.

cryosurgery: A surgical technique using extreme cold to destroy tumors.

deoxyribonucleic acid (DNA): The molecules inside cells that carry genetic information and pass it from one generation to the next.

genes: The basic units of genetic material found in the nucleus of the cell.

immunotherapy: A treatment aimed at strengthening the patient's immune system and helping it recognize cancer cells as foreign.

leukemia: A type of cancer that affects the blood.

lymphoma: A cancer of the lymph nodes.

malignant: The designation of a tumor that is cancerous.

metastasis: The spread of cancer cells to different parts of the body, where they form new tumors.

mutation: A chemical change in a gene, which may produce a new trait that can be inherited.

oncogenes: Genes that may give rise to cancer.

proteins: Molecules made of amino acids that the body needs to function.

remission: A lessening or disappearance of disease symptoms.

sarcoma: A type of cancer that originates in muscle cells and connective tissue.

stem cells: Primitive cells that can develop into different cell types.

suppressor genes: Genes that help control cell growth and division.

tumor: An abnormal (benign or malignant) mass of tissue that arises without an obvious cause.

Organizations to Contact

American Institute for Cancer Research (AICR)

1759 R St. NW
Washington, DC 20009
phone: (800) 843-8114
fax: (202) 328-7226
Web site: www.aicr.org
e-mail: aicrweb@aicr.org

The American Institute for Cancer Research provides information about cancer prevention, particularly through diet and nutrition. It offers a toll-free nutrition hotline and a pen-pal support network, and it funds research grants. Publications in Spanish are available.

Cancer Care, Inc.

275 Seventh Ave.
New York, NY 10001
phone: (800) 813-4673
fax: (212) 712-8495
Web site: www.cancercare.org
e-mail: info@cancercare.org

This national nonprofit agency offers free support, information, financial assistance, and practical help to people with cancer. Services are provided by oncology social workers and are available in person, over the phone, and through the agency's Web site.

Cancer Information and Counseling Line (CICL)

AMC Cancer Research Center
1600 Pierce St.

Denver, CO 80214
phone: (800) 525-3777
Web site: www.amc.org/counseling/index.html
e-mail: ciclhelp@amc.org

The CICL is a toll-free service for cancer patients, their family members and friends, cancer survivors, and the general public. Professional counselors provide up-to-date medical information, emotional support through short-term counseling, and resource referrals to callers nationwide. Questions about cancer and requests for resources may also be submitted through e-mail.

Cancer Information Service

National Cancer Institute
9000 Rockville Pike
Building 31, Room 10A16
Bethesda, MD 20892
phone: (800) 4-CANCER
Web site: http://cis.nci.nih.gov

At this nationwide network founded by the National Cancer Institute, trained cancer information specialists answer virtually any question on cancer. The CIS outreach coordinator is available to groups to help set up educational programs.

I Can Cope

American Cancer Society
1599 Clifton Rd. NE
Atlanta, GA 30329-4251
phone: (800) 227-2345
Web site: www.cancer.org/docroot/ESN/content/ESN_3_1X_I_Can_Cope.asp

This educational program for people facing cancer offers help in the form of reliable information, peer support, and practical coping skills. I Can Cope classes are taught by doctors, nurses, social workers, and other health care professional or community representatives.

Vital Options International TeleSupport Cancer Network

15821 Ventura Blvd., Suite 645
Encino, CA 91436-2946
phone: (800) 477-7666
Web site: www.vitaloptions.org
e-mail: info@vitaloptions.org

Vital Options uses communications technology to reach people dealing with cancer through a weekly syndicated call-in radio talk show on cancer called "The Group Room," which provides a forum for patients, long-term survivors, family members, physicians, and therapists to discuss cancer issues.

The Wellness Community

35 E. Seventh St., Suite 412
Cincinnati, OH 45202
phone: (888) 793-9355
Web site: www.thewellnesscommunity.org
e-mail: help@wellness-community.org

This organization provides free psychological and emotional support to cancer patients and their families. It offers support groups on stress reduction and cancer education workshops, nutrition guidance, exercise sessions, and social events.

For Further Reading

Books

Lance Armstrong with Sally Jenkins, *It's Not About the Bike: My Journey Back to Life*. New York: Putnam, 2000. Professional cyclist Lance Armstrong tells the story of his struggle with cancer and the physical and emotional problems he encountered.

Wilma R. Caldwell, ed., *Cancer Information for Teens*. Detroit: Omnigraphics, 2004. This book contains health tips about cancer awareness, prevention, diagnosis, and treatment. It also contains facts about frequently occurring cancers, cancer risk factors, and coping strategies for teens fighting cancer or dealing with cancer in family members or friends.

ZoAnn Dreyer, *Living with Cancer*. New York: Facts On File, 2008. This book explains what the medical community knows about cancer and what patients can expect during cancer treatments. The author gives advice on preventing cancer and suggests ways to handle the emotional trauma when a loved one develops cancer. The book contains a number of helpful appendixes listing organizations that can provide resources and support for cancer patients and their families.

Paraic A. Kenny, *Stages of Cancer Development*. New York: Chelsea House, 2007. This book is one in a series on the biology of cancer. After viewing cancer from a historical perspective, the author traces the ways cancer develops and progresses and the types of treatment available. There are brief profiles of some of the scientists who have pioneered cancer research, and the book contains a number of helpful illustrations.

Alvin and Virginia Silverstein and Laura Silverstein Nunn, *Cancer*. Minneapolis: Twenty First Century Books, 2006. The authors explain the different types of cancer, their causes, symptoms, and treatment. Case studies reveal what it is like to live with cancer.

NCI Booklets

The National Cancer Institute issues a series of booklets about specific types of cancer, which are updated regularly. Each booklet provides information on the symptoms, diagnosis, treatment, emotional issues, and questions to ask the doctor about that kind of cancer. Other NCI booklets containing more general advice for cancer patients include: *Eating Hints for Cancer Patients, Taking Part in Clinical Trials: What Cancer Patients Need to Know, Facing Forward: Life After Cancer Treatment, When Cancer Returns*, and *Coping with Advanced Cancer*. The National Cancer Institute booklets can be obtained from the NCI Cancer Information Service by calling (800) 4-CANCER.

Web Sites

American Cancer Society (ACS) (www.cancer.org). The ACS offers a variety of services to cancer patients and their families. It also supports research, provides printed materials, and conducts educational programs.

Lance Armstrong Foundation (www.livestrong.org). This nonprofit organization founded by cancer survivor Lance Armstrong provides resources and support services to people diagnosed with cancer. It also includes first-person stories from cancer survivors.

Look Good . . . Feel Better for Teens (www.lookgoodfeel better.org/audience/teens/program.htm). This hospital-based public service program helps teenagers from ages thirteen to seventeen deal with their appearance, their health, and the social side effects of cancer treatment. The program offers on-site sessions in some sixteen cities as well as the 2bMe Web site (www.2bme.org/2bMe.html) to reach teens everywhere.

National Cancer Institute (NCI) (www.cancer.gov). The NCI provides accurate, up-to-date information on many kinds of cancer, and it houses various resources for people dealing with cancer.

Index

normal, 15
Cervical cancer, 22, 29
Chemotherapy, 26, 33–35, *34*, 74–75
Chernobyl nuclear power plant, *46*, 47
Chewing tobacco, 40–41
Children
  Burkitt's lymphoma, *48*
  cigarettes ads and, 40
  hepatitis B virus (HBV), 49
  leukemia and, 16, 52, 59, 72
  resources for, 36, 70, 72
  secondhand smoke and, 42
  survivors, 59–61
Chondroblastic osteosarcoma, 61–63
Cigarettes. *See* Smoking
Cigars, 40
Colon cancer, *10*, *14*
Complementary medicine, 37, *85*, 85–86
Crawford, Cindy, 72
Cryosurgery/cryotherapy, 33
Curie, Irene, 44
Curie, Marie, 44
Curie, Pierre, 44
Cycle of Hope, 57

D
Daffodil Days, 57–58, *58*, 68
Dalzell, Michael, 12
Deaths
  annually, 6
  by gender and type of cancer, *17*
  lifestyle and, 53
  from radon gas, 44
  from smoking, 38–39
Designer drugs, 77–78
Detection
  biopsies, 31–32, *32*
  characteristics of successful programs, 28–29
  genetic testing, 18–19
  mammograms, 18, *19*, 29
  number of new cases annually, 6
  self-examinations, 26–28
  survival and, 23
  types of screening tests, 29

See also Symptoms
Diet, 8, 50–52, *51*, 53–54
DNA (deoxyribonucleic acid)
  described, 10–11, *11*
  effect of radiation therapy on, 73
  research, 81–83
  viruses and, 48
Dogs, 20
Dronabinol, 75
Drugs. *See* Chemotherapy

E
Edwards, Elizabeth, 55
Electro-acupuncture, 75
Embryonic stem cells, 87
Endoscopes, 31
Energy levels, 25, *25*
Epstein-Barr virus (EBV), 22, 49
Exercise, 8, 52–53, *53*

F
Familial cancers, 18

G
Gardasil, 50
Gastrointestinal tumors (GIST), 76
Gender, *17*
Genes
  described, 10–11
  multiplication of cells and, 13
  mutated, 18–19
  research, 81–83, *82*
  treatment and, 12, 77–78
"Genetic Medicine: Powerful Opportunities for Good and Greed" (Dalzell), 12
Genetic testing, 18–19
Genomics, 12
Gleevec, 75–76, *77*
"Good News About Cancer" (Basler), 22

H
Hair loss, 36
Halligan, Kate, 20
Hamilton, Scott, 27
Heart disease, 6
Hepatitis B virus (HBV), 48, 49

Picture Credits

About the Author

Elizabeth Silverthorne has written more than twenty books as well as short stories and articles for adults and children. Her father and her husband were physicians. Her son was in medical school when he was diagnosed with Hodgkin's disease, and after a brave fight, he died at the age of twenty-four. A former college teacher, Elizabeth lives in the small village of Salado in the heart of Texas.